COOKING AROUND THE WORLD:

CHICKEN AND FISH

Including vegetables, grains, salads, breads
and desserts

mary bayramian

illustrated by richard w. roesener

TROUBADOR PRESS   SAN FRANCISCO

In Dedication

To my husband Jack, for his love of good eating.

Library of Congress Cataloging in Publication Data

Bayramian, Mary, 1921–
  Cooking around the world.

  Includes index.
  1. Cookery (Chicken)   2. Cookery (Fish)
3. Cookery, International. I. Title.
TX750.B38   641.6'6'5   77-11060
ISBN 0-912300-85-X

Published in the United States of America by
TROUBADOR PRESS
385 Fremont Street
San Francisco, California 94105

Contents

Acknowledgement

In our travels throughout the world, many were generous in sharing their delicious recipes. To them all my deep felt thanks and appreciation.

Metric Conversions

Weight

1 pound (16-ounces)	448 grams (g)
½ pound (8-ounces)	224 grams
¼ pound (4-ounces)	112 grams
(1-ounce)	28 grams

Volume

1 teaspoon (1/9 fl. ounce)	5 milliliters (mL)
1 tablespoon (⅓ fl. ounce)	15 milliliters
1 cup (8 fl. ounces)	0.24 liters (L)
1 pint (16 fl. ounces)	0.47 liters
1 quart (32 fl. ounces)	0.95 liters

Length

1 inch	2.54 centimeters (cm)

Temperature

32° Fahrenheit (freezing point of water)	0° Celsius (C)
212° Fahrenheit (boiling point of water)	100° Celsius

Introduction

For varied reasons, many people forsake the typical red meat-laden diet. Some as a way to reduce their cholesterol and saturated fat intake, some over concern for drugs used in raising animals for food, others for philosophical or religious reasons. When this diet change is made the first question is "where do I get my protein"? Fish and chicken are rich in protein along with many of the legumes, nuts and seeds, grains and vegetables. This book provides over 200 recipes using these delicious, nutritious foods.

Throughout the world fish and chicken are prepared in a variety of interesting ways and can provide the basis for many imaginative meals. During the last two decades people in the United States have become far less traditional in their eating patterns and far more eager to experience international cuisine. Whatever cultural or regional differences separate people, it may be said we all share a fondness for tasteful and wholesome food. National and regional recipes and cooking traditions are highly cherished and passed on to succeeding generations.

Traveling provided me interesting and wonderful opportunities to taste, compare and enjoy many ethnic foods. These recipes will provide you the chance to experience and enjoy varied fish and chicken specialities from around the world.

Note: slight adaptations and substitutions of spices, herbs and ingredients in recipes should of course be made to suit your tastes. Unless otherwise stated, all recipes serve four.

fish and seafood

In many countries fish and seafood are staple foods. The seas, streams and lakes of the world yield a plentiful variety of fish— over 20,000 species. When any variety of fish is prepared and cooked with care it is delicious. The cook determines choice by flavor and texture. We are all familiar with the traditional ways of preparing fish and seafood: baked, broiled, poached and fried. Aside from these methods, there are many other possibilities, as shown in this section. Inventive cooks have created innumerable recipes for preparing fish using subtle seasonings and various ingredients, primarily vegetables.

Fish is an easily digestible, low calorie, high-protein food. A pound of lean white fish has under 350 calories, compared to a pound of beef that has 1,400 calories.

The recipes contained in this section run the gamut from quick and easy, to elegant and festive, offering you an adventuresome variety in the preparation and enjoyment of fish and seafood.

Buying Fish

Fresh fish should have reddish-pink gills; scales should be bright in color and adhere closely to the body; the eyes bulging, bright and clear. There should be no strong "fishy" odor and the flesh must be firm, springing back when pressed.

FISH TERMS

Whole fish   as it comes out of the water.

Drawn fish   whole, but eviscerated.

Dressed fish   whole, but eviscerated and scaled. Normally with head, tail and fins removed. (Pan-dressed fish refers to smaller fish, less than 1 pound.)

Steaks   cross-section slices cut from large dressed fish, ¾-inch to 1-inch thick.

Fillets   sides or parts of the fish, cut lengthwise and boned, with all or most of the skin removed.

Storing Fish

Wrap in foil or waxed paper tightly to remove air and refrigerate in the coldest section. Many prefer freezer for storage beyond a day or two. Fresh fish should be used the day it is purchased.

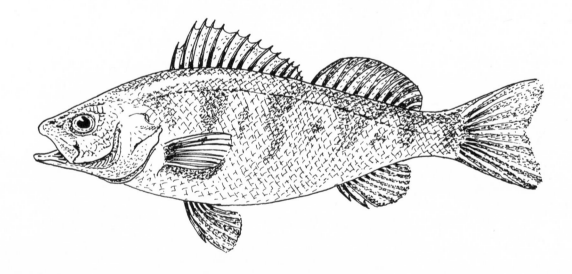

Fish and Seafood

This is a Cajun recipe for shrimp Jambalaya from New Orleans

CAJUN SHRIMP JAMBALAYA

4 T oil
3 T flour
2 medium onions, chopped
1 medium green bell pepper, chopped
1 garlic clove, finely minced
1 cup tomato sauce
2 cups water
2 cups cooked cleaned shrimp
1 t salt
½ t black pepper
2 cups cooked rice
¼ cup finely minced parsley
¼ cup thinly sliced green onion tops

In a heavy saucepan heat oil; add flour and brown very lightly. Add onion, green pepper and garlic; cook until onions are soft. Add tomato sauce, water, shrimp, salt and pepper; simmer for 30 minutes. Add cooked rice and simmer 5 minutes longer; taste for seasoning. Spoon onto serving platter. Sprinkle with parsley and onion tops.

A traditional Southern United States specialty; gumbo made with shrimp, tomatoes, okra and rice

SHRIMP GUMBO

2 medium onions, chopped
4 T vinegar
1 lb. uncooked shrimp, washed
4 cups boiling water
1½ t butter
1½ t flour
2 cups fresh sliced okra
½ cup cooked rice
3 large tomatoes, peeled and chopped
1 bay leaf
⅛ t salt
⅛ t black pepper

Add half of onion, vinegar, and shrimp to boiling water. Cook until shrimp is pink, about 15 minutes. Remove shrimp, shell and devein; save stock. Sauté remaining onion in butter; blend in flour and add okra. Add rice, tomatoes, bay leaf, salt and pepper; mix thoroughly, then add shrimp and reserved stock. Simmer until okra and tomatoes are cooked. Remove bay leaf and taste for seasoning.

3

The Arabs create a most unusual dressing to stuff a fish, made of walnuts and pomegranates, called Samakah Harrah

BAKED FISH WITH WALNUT AND POMEGRANATE STUFFING

1 4-lb.-whole striped bass or any whole, firm, white fish
4 T olive oil
2 t salt

Clean and scale fish leaving on head and tail. Season fish with salt (inside and out); lay flat in a shallow baking dish. Pour olive oil over fish and marinate for 15 minutes. Fill fish with walnut-pomegranate stuffing and close opening with small skewers. Bake in a 400° preheated oven for 40 to 50 minutes, basting fish every 15 minutes with accumulated cooking juices. The fish is cooked when it feels firm to the touch. Do not overcook. Carefully remove fish to a warm serving platter.

Walnut and Pomegranate Stuffing:

1 cup finely chopped onion
4 T olive oil
1½ cup finely chopped green pepper
1 cup ground walnuts
1 T finely chopped parsley
2 T fresh pomegranate seeds
1 t salt
1½ t freshly ground black pepper

In a heavy skillet sauté onions in olive oil, stirring frequently, for 10 minutes. Stir in green pepper and walnuts; cook another few minutes until peppers are soft. Turn heat off, add parsley, pomegranate, salt and pepper.

Garnish:

1 lemon, cut in thin slices
2 T fresh pomegranate seeds
½ cup finely chopped parsley

Garnish top of fish with a row of lemon slices. Sprinkle with parsley and pomegranate seeds. If desired, serve extra wedges of lemon.

Egyptian Kammooniyya, fish fillets baked with tomatoes, onions and spices, served with rice

BAKED FISH WITH TOMATOES AND RICE

2 large onions, sliced ¼-inch thick
2 garlic cloves, finely minced
1 t cumin
6 T vegetable oil
1 cup finely chopped celery
½ cup tomato puree
1 cup water
1½ t salt
¼ t freshly ground black pepper
4 white fish fillets, about ½ lb. each
1 large tomato, thinly sliced
2 cups hot cooked rice

In a large skillet, cook and stir onions, garlic and cumin in 4 tablespoons oil until golden brown, about 6-7 minutes. With slotted spoon remove onion and set aside. Add celery to skillet, stir frequently. Return onions and stir in tomato puree, water, ½ teaspoon salt, and black pepper. Stir while simmering until mixture is thickened and most of the liquid has evaporated. Remove from heat. Brush shallow baking dish with 1 tablespoon oil; arrange fish in single layer and sprinkle with 1 teaspoon salt. Spread sauce evenly over fish; top with tomato slices and sprinkle with 1 tablespoon oil. Cover tightly and bake in a 350° preheated oven for 20 minutes. Remove cover and bake 15 minutes longer. Arrange fish on large platter around rice and garnish with remaining sauce.

Easy to prepare, yet superb in flavor and taste is the New Orleans style of baked salmon

BAKED SALMON NEW ORLEANS

1 garlic clove
1 small dried red pepper pod
2 lb. piece of salmon
⅛ t salt
⅛ t black pepper
1 medium onion, finely minced
1 t sugar
2½ cups stewed tomatoes
1 T Worcestershire sauce
6 T olive oil
1 T vinegar
2 cups uncooked potato balls, scooped from peeled whole
   potatoes
1 cup sliced fresh mushrooms

Put garlic and red pepper pod inside salmon and set in baking dish; season with salt, pepper, onion and sugar. Cover with tomatoes; add Worcestershire sauce, olive oil, vinegar and potatoes. Bake in 400° preheated oven for 15 minutes. Add mushrooms and bake until tender, approximately 15 minutes.

A typical way Romanians prepare their baked fish is with vegetables

BAKED FISH WITH VEGETABLES

2 medium onions, thinly sliced
1 garlic clove, crushed
2 leeks, white part only in 1-inch slices
⅓ cup olive oil
½ cup diced carrots
½ cup green beans, cut in 1-inch pieces
3 medium tomatoes, peeled and chopped
3 T chopped fresh dill weed
⅓ cup chopped parsley
¼ cup seedless raisins
2 T lemon juice
¼ t black pepper
1 t salt
2 lbs. fish, slices or fillets

Sauté onions, garlic and leeks in olive oil until soft. Add carrots, green beans and tomatoes. Sauté 5 minutes. Add dill, parsley, raisins, lemon juice, pepper and salt. Place fish in a shallow baking dish and spread evenly with sauce. Bake, covered, in a 350° preheated oven until tender, about 30 minutes. minutes.

Salsa Di Vongoli, a delicious clam sauce served over pasta, Italian style

CLAM SAUCE OVER PASTA

2 small garlic cloves, finely minced
2 t olive oil
4 T minced parsley
1 cup minced clams
½ cup clam juice
⅓ cup tomato sauce
¼ cup medium sherry
¼ t salt
Freshly ground black pepper
8 ounces spaghetti or other pasta, cooked to taste

Sauté garlic in olive oil until softened. Add parsley, clams and clam juice. Stir in tomato sauce and sherry. Simmer over low heat, about 10 minutes. Add salt and dash of freshly ground black pepper. Serve over hot cooked pasta. If desired, sprinkle generously with Parmesan cheese.

Here is a delicious crab-avocado cutlet we first tasted in Mazatlan, Mexico

CRAB-AVOCADO CUTLETS

3 T butter
4 T flour
½ t salt
⅛ t black pepper
1½ cups milk
2 cups diced avocado
2 cups cooked crab meat
3 eggs, beaten
Fine dried bread crumbs
Oil for frying

Melt butter and blend in flour. Add salt, pepper and milk; cook until thickened, stirring constantly. Add avocado and crab meat; mix well. Cool mixture. Shape into 8 cutlets and roll in crumbs, then in egg and again in crumbs. In a large skillet, heat oil and brown cutlets on both sides. Serve immediately.

Thick and hearty New England clam chowder originated in the American Northeast where frugal folk took what was at hand and created a classic

NEW ENGLAND CLAM CHOWDER

2 T butter
1 small onion, diced
½ cup diced celery
2 cups cubed uncooked potatoes
2 cups water
½ t salt
¼ t black pepper
2 cups milk
1 cup minced clams
Paprika

Melt butter; add onion and celery. Cook until tender but not browned. Add potatoes, water, salt and pepper. Cover and simmer until potato is tender, about 15 minutes. Add milk and clams; heat. Serve in warmed bowls and sprinkle with paprika.

One of the ways Romanians prepare a whole fish is with an olive stuffing and baked with onions and lemons

OLIVE STUFFED FISH

1 3-lb. whole carp or white-fleshed fish
2 t salt
2 medium onions, sliced
1 lemon, sliced
½ t black pepper
¼ cup dry bread crumbs
3 T olive oil
¼ cup hot water

After washing and drying fish, sprinkle inside and out with 1 teaspoon salt. Fill fish cavity with olive stuffing. Arrange onions and lemon slices evenly in a baking dish, place fish over. Sprinkle with 1 teaspoon salt, pepper and bread crumbs. Mix olive oil and hot water; spoon over fish. Bake in a 400° preheated oven until fork-tender, about 30 minutes.

Olive Stuffing:

1 cup chopped green olives
1 garlic clove, finely minced
2 T lemon juice
¼ cup chopped parsley
1 T olive oil

In a bowl combine olives, garlic, lemon juice, parsley and olive oil. Mix thoroughly.

In the resort town of Acapulco, Mexico, this very simple and delicious salad of crab and avocado is a most satisfying luncheon

CRAB AND AVOCADO SALAD

½ cup mayonnaise
½ cup catsup
½ cup dry sherry
2 t lemon juice
Dash of cayenne pepper
3 cups crab meat, diced and chilled
2 cups diced avocado
1 cup finely diced celery
Crisp lettuce leaves

In a bowl mix mayonnaise, catsup, sherry, lemon juice and dash of cayenne; blend thoroughly. Chill for 1 hour. Shortly before serving, gently toss together crab, avocado, celery and dressing. On a platter, or individual plates, arrange crisp lettuce leaves and heap on salad. If desired, decorate with wedges of hard-boiled eggs and olives.

A delicious, easy to prepare California casserole of crab, noodles, mushrooms and wine

CRAB AND NOODLES

1 medium onion, sliced
3 T butter
1½ cup sliced fresh mushrooms
3 T tomato puree
1 cup dry white wine
1 t salt
⅛ t black pepper
4 T grated Gruyère cheese
5 T Parmesan cheese
2 cups shredded crabmeat
2 T chopped parsley
3 cups cooked and drained noodles

Sauté onions in 2 tablespoons butter until soft; do not allow to brown. Add mushrooms and sauté 5 minutes. Add tomato puree, wine, salt and pepper; cook gently for a few minutes. Stir in Gruyère cheese and 4 tablespoons Parmesan cheese; heat until cheese is melted. Remove from heat; add crabmeat and parsley. Add cooked noodles to crab mixture. Spoon into a buttered casserole and sprinkle with 1 tablespoon Parmesan cheese. Dot with remaining butter and bake in a 350° preheated oven for 25 minutes.

Cauliflower Shrimp Newburg is just a little out of the ordinary. Cauliflower, topped with shrimp in a sherry-flavored cream sauce. A European delight

CAULIFLOWER SHRIMP NEWBURG

1 large fresh cauliflower, broken into flowerettes
3 T butter
3 T flour
1 cup milk
½ cup half and half
1 t salt
¼ t mace
3 T tomato paste
3 T dry sherry
1 T lemon juice
1 t paprika
1½ cups cooked small shrimp
¼ t freshly ground pepper
2 T finely minced parsley

Cook cauliflower until tender but firm. Place in a serving bowl and keep hot. Melt butter in a saucepan over low heat. Add flour and cook, stirring for 2 minutes. Blend in milk, half and half, salt and mace. Cook and stir until mixture boils and thickens. Blend in tomato paste, sherry, lemon juice and paprika. Add shrimp and pepper; heat through. Pour sauce over cauliflower and sprinkle with parsley.

Coquilles Saint-Jacques is a delicate French preparation of scallops with wine and mushrooms in a sauce

CREAMED SCALLOPS WITH MUSHROOMS

1 lb. scallops, cut in small pieces
1½ cups water
¾ cup dry white wine
6 sprigs parsley
1 bay leaf
6 T butter
3 T flour
2 egg yolks, slightly beaten
4 T cream
1½ cups diced mushrooms
1 cup finely chopped onion
2 T dry sherry
1 t lemon juice
1¼ t salt
1 t freshly ground black pepper
½ cup dry bread crumbs

Combine in a saucepan, scallops, water, white wine, 2 sprigs parsley and bay leaf. Bring to a boil, reduce heat and simmer until tender, about 5 minutes. Remove parsley and bay leaf, drain scallops and reserve liquid. In a saucepan melt 3 tablespoons butter and blend in flour. Add reserved liquid from scallops, stirring constantly, bring to a boil. Simmer 3 minutes. In a small bowl mix together egg yolk and cream. Add a few spoons of hot mixture, stirring steadily to prevent curdling. Add to remaining sauce and cook until mixture thickens; do not allow to boil. Remove from heat. In a second saucepan combine mushrooms, onions, sherry, lemon juice and 2 tablespoons butter. Cover and cook 10 minutes. Combine sauce and mushroom-onion mixture. Add scallops, salt and pepper; mix thoroughly. Spoon in scallop shells or ramekins. Cover with bread crumbs and dot with remaining 1 tablespoon butter. Bake in a 425° preheated oven for 10 minutes. Garnish each with a sprig of parsley.

Istanbul, Turkey is noted for the way broiled skewered swordfish is prepared, especially delicious when cooked over a bed of hot coals

BROILED SKEWERED SWORDFISH

1 small onion, sliced and separated into rings
4 T lemon juice
4 t olive oil
2 t salt
½ t freshly ground black pepper
1½ lbs. swordfish, sliced 1-inch thick
20 large bay leaves
2 cups boiling water
4 medium tomatoes, cut in half
1 large green bell pepper, cut in 2-inch squares

In a deep bowl, combine into a marinade onions, 2 tablespoons lemon juice, 2 teaspoons olive oil, salt and pepper. Skin and bone swordfish slices and cut into 1-inch cubes. Add to the marinade, gently tossing swordfish to coat well. Marinate at room temperature for 2 hours, turning fish occasionally. Place bay leaves in a bowl, pour water over and soak for 1 hour. Meanwhile, light a layer of coals in a charcoal broiler and let burn until a white ash appears on the surface, or preheat a stove broiler to its highest point. On 4 skewers string cubes of fish and drained bay leaves alternately, pressing them firmly together. On 2 other skewers alternately string tomatoes and green pepper. Combine remaining 2 tablespoons lemon juice and 2 teaspoons oil; brush mixture evenly over fish. Broil 3-inches from heat, turning skewers occasionally for 10 minutes or until fish is golden brown and tomatoes are soft. Excellent served with rice pilaf.

Bouillabaisse, a stew-soup originated in Marseilles, France, usually served with chunks of crusty French bread and a glass of good white wine

BOUILLABAISSE

1 leek, cut in 1-inch slices
1 medium onion, chopped
1 garlic clove, finely minced
2 large tomatoes, peeled and chopped
½ cup olive oil
1 bay leaf
2 t chopped parsley
1 t salt
½ t freshly ground black pepper
1 t paprika
¼ t saffron
2 cups clam juice
2 cups water
2 lbs. assorted fish, such as bass, haddock, snapper or flounder, cut in 2-inch thick slices
2 lbs. assorted shellfish, such as shrimp, scallops, crab or lobster cut in large chunks
1 cup dry white wine

In a large saucepan sauté leek, onion, garlic and tomatoes in olive oil. Add bay leaf, parsley, salt, pepper, paprika, saffron, clam juice and water; bring to a boil. Add fish and simmer 10 minutes. Add shellfish and wine and boil 10 minutes longer. Taste. Add salt if necessary. Traditionally served with slices of French bread rubbed with freshly cut garlic.

A hearty meal, Norwegian Cod and Potato Casserole

COD AND POTATO CASSEROLE

1½ lbs. cod fillets
4 T lemon juice
1 t salt
½ t black pepper
6 medium potatoes, peeled and thinly sliced
2 T butter
1 medium onion, finely chopped
2 T chopped parsley
3 T dried bread crumbs

Wash and dry cod fillets. Place in a single layer in a buttered shallow oven dish. Sprinkle with lemon juice, salt and pepper. Place sliced potatoes in a layer over cod. Dot with butter and bake in a 450° preheated oven for 15 minutes. Sprinkle with onions, parsley and bread crumbs. Continue baking for another 15 minutes or until potatoes are tender.

A hearty dish for a cold night, Norwegian Cod Stew

COD STEW

1 cup diced Brussels sprouts
½ cup diced celery
1 leek, diced
4 medium potatoes, peeled and diced
4 carrots, diced
2 cups milk
1 t salt
½ t black pepper
1 lb. cod fillets, cut in chunks
1 T butter
2 T flour
4 T chopped parsley

Combine Brussels sprouts, celery, leek, potatoes and carrots in a large saucepan. Add milk, salt and pepper. Cover and cook until vegetables are almost tender. Add cod and simmer another 10 minutes. In a saucepan melt butter and stir in flour; add milky liquid drained from vegetables and cod. Simmer for 10 minutes, stirring constantly. Mix sauce with fish and vegetables. Add parsley and taste for seasoning; add if necessary. Simmer slowly until well heated.

An elegant Swedish style rolled fillet of sole covered with crab and mushrooms in a cream sauce

FILLET OF SOLE WITH CRAB

1 lb. fillet of sole (4 fillets)
1½ cup sliced fresh mushrooms
3 T butter
½ cup flaked crab meat
2 T flour
1 cup cream
½ t salt
¼ t black pepper
2 T grated Parmesan cheese
¼ cup dried bread crumbs
Paprika

Wash and dry fillet of sole. Sauté mushrooms lightly in 2 tablespoons butter. Add crab meat and sprinkle with flour. Stir and gradually add cream, continue stirring until sauce has thickened. Add salt and pepper. In each of four individual baking dishes that have been buttered, stand a fish fillet on its side, so that it forms a circle. Carefully spoon sauce equally into each circle. Bake in a 400° preheated oven for 10 minutes. Remove from oven and sprinkle with cheese, bread crumbs and a dash of paprika. Top each with part of remaining butter. Place under broiler until golden brown and cheese is melted.

West African Ntorewafroe, a fish and eggplant stew enhanced with green pepper, onion and tomato

EGGPLANT AND FISH STEW

1 lb. fish fillets
3 T oil
1 medium eggplant, pared and cut in 1-inch cubes
¾ cup chopped onion
¾ cup chopped green bell pepper
2 cups peeled and chopped tomatoes
1 cup chicken broth
1 t salt
Dash of cayenne pepper

In a large skillet quickly sauté fish in oil. Remove and set aside. To same skillet add eggplant, onion and green pepper. Cook until vegetables are tender but not brown, about 15 minutes. Add tomatoes, chicken broth, salt and cayenne pepper. Cover and simmer about 15 minutes, stirring occasionally. Break fish fillets into large pieces and place on top of eggplant and tomato mixture. Taste for seasoning and add salt if necessary. Cover and cook another 5 minutes. Best served with cooked rice.

The French prepare a shrimp and hard-boiled egg salad, simple yet elegant for a cool summer lunch

COLD SHRIMP REMOULADE

3 hard-boiled eggs
½ t dry mustard
1 t anchovy paste
1 cup mayonnaise
⅓ cup Burgundy wine
1 T finely minced onion
2 cups cooked small shrimp
1 cup diced celery
2 T finely minced parsley
Lettuce leaves
Paprika

Mash yolk of eggs with mustard and anchovy paste. Blend in mayonnaise, wine and onion. Add shrimp, celery and parsley. Serve on lettuce leaves and top with finely minced egg white and paprika.

Armenian Fish Plaki is prepared with fish fillets baked with a topping of sautéed vegetables.

FISH PLAKI

2 medium onions, peeled and sliced
1 garlic clove, finely minced
6 T olive oil
3 medium tomatoes, peeled and chopped
2 medium carrots, thinly sliced
2 stalks celery, sliced
1 t salt
½ t freshly ground black pepper
2 lbs. fish fillets
2 large lemons, sliced
3 T finely minced parsley

In a large skillet, sauté onions and garlic in oil until soft. Add tomatoes, carrots, celery, salt and pepper; cook for 5 minutes. Arrange fish fillets in a shallow baking dish and cover with vegetable mixture. Arrange lemon slices over them. Sprinkle with parsley. Bake in a 350° preheated oven until fish is fork-tender, about 20 minutes. This may be served either hot or cold.

The Russians prepare an interesting baked fish stuffed with buckwheat groats and topped with sour cream

BUCKWHEAT GROATS STUFFED FISH

4 whole white-fleshed fish, about 1 lb. each
1 t salt
¼ t black pepper
2 T butter
½ cup fine dry bread crumbs
¾ cup sour cream

Arrange fish in a shallow baking dish and sprinkle cavities with salt and pepper; fill with buckwheat stuffing. Melt butter and spoon over fish; sprinkle with bread crumbs. Bake in a 400° preheated oven, until fish is tender, about 20 minutes. Spoon sour cream over fish and cook another 5 minutes.

Buckwheat Stuffing:

1 medium onion, finely chopped
2 T butter
1 cup cooked, crushed buckwheat groats
1 hard-boiled egg, chopped
2 T chopped parsley
1 T chopped fresh dill weed
½ t salt
¼ t black pepper

Sauté onions in butter. Add buckwheat, egg, parsley, dill, salt and pepper. Mix well.

Quick and easy to prepare is crab with Chinese cabbage, flavored with onion, sherry and ginger

CRAB MEAT WITH CHINESE CABBAGE

2 T oil
4 green onions, thinly sliced
1 T dry sherry
½ t salt
½ t sugar
¼ t powdered ginger
1 Chinese cabbage, cut in 1-inch pieces
1 cup chicken broth
1½ T cornstarch
2 T water
1 cup flaked crab meat

Heat oil in skillet, add onions, sherry, salt, sugar and ginger; cook for 1 minute. Add cabbage and chicken broth. Cover and simmer until tender but crisp, about 5 minutes. Blend cornstarch and water; add to cabbage. Cook and stir until thickened. Add crab and heat through. This may be served over Chinese noodles or rice.

Easy to prepare, yet with a gourmet flavor, tuna with asparagus and almonds baked in a sauce

TUNA WITH ASPARAGUS AND ALMONDS

4 T butter
2 T flour
1 cup milk
1 egg yolk, slightly beaten
4 T cream
1 t lemon juice
1 cup tuna, drained of oil
6 T slivered almonds
½ t salt
⅛ t black pepper
¼ t mace
20 cooked large asparagus spears
2 t chopped parsley

In a saucepan melt 2 tablespoons of butter and stir in flour. Add milk a little at a time, stirring constantly; cook for 5 minutes. Mix egg yolk with cream and lemon juice; stir gradually into sauce. Add tuna, 4 tablespoons of almonds, salt, pepper and mace. Arrange asparagus in a baking dish; cover with tuna mixture. Sprinkle with remaining almonds and dot with 2 tablespoons butter. Bake in a 350° preheated oven for 30 minutes. Sprinkle with chopped parsley and serve.

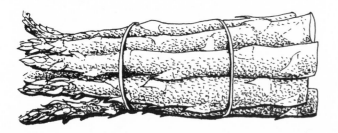

Here is a Basque specialty, Truchas a la Navarra, trout baked in red wine and herbs

TROUT BAKED IN RED WINE

½ cup dry red wine
4 T olive oil
4 T water
½ cup finely chopped onion
1 T finely cut fresh mint or ½ t dried mint
½ t dried rosemary
½ t dried thyme
1 bay leaf, crumbled
12 whole black peppercorns
1 t salt
4 trout, about 1 lb. each
3 egg yolks, slightly beaten
1 T finely minced parsley

In a flameproof baking dish, large enough to hold trout in one layer; combine wine, olive oil, water, onions, mint, rosemary, thyme, bay leaf, peppercorns and salt, stir thoroughly. Place trout in marinade and spoon mixture over. Marinate at room temperature for 30 minutes, basting occasionally. On top of the stove bring marinated trout to a simmer; turn flame off and cover baking dish loosely with foil. Bake in 350° preheated oven for 20 minutes or until fish is firm to the touch. With a slotted spatula, transfer trout to a heated serving platter and keep warm. Strain cooking liquid into a saucepan through a fine sieve, pressing onions and herbs with the back of a spoon before discarding. Mix a little cooking liquid into egg yolks; beat this into remaining liquid in saucepan. Heat slowly, stirring until sauce thickens slightly. Do not allow to boil or sauce will curdle. Pour sauce over trout and sprinkle with minced parsley. Traditionally the trout is served with hot boiled potatoes.

A traditional favorite is Israeli gefilte fish, ovals of ground fish, onion, carrot and matzo meal

GEFILTE FISH

2 medium carrots, thinly sliced
1 cup chopped onion
6 cups water
⅛ t black pepper
3 t salt
1½ lbs. pike fillets, skinned and boned
2 eggs
2 T ice water
2 T matzo meal
Lettuce leaves
Red horseradish
Pickles

In a saucepan combine half the carrots, half the onion, water, pepper and 2 teaspoons salt. Bring to a boil and simmer uncovered for 30 minutes. Finely grind raw fish and remaining carrots and onions. Place in a bowl; add eggs, ice water, matzo meal and 1 teaspoon salt. Beat at high speed with an electric mixer until fluffy. Shape into ovals, using ¼ cup for each. Carefully add to vegetable-water mixture, cover and simmer 20 minutes. Drain, reserving fish and carrots. Cool, cover and chill. When ready to serve, place gefilte fish on lettuce and sprinkle with carrots. Serve with red horseradish and pickles.

An easy to prepare Swedish style of halibut baked on a bed of mushrooms, onions, carrots and wine

HALIBUT ON A BED OF VEGETABLES

2 cups thinly sliced carrots
6 T butter
1 large onion, chopped
½ cup chopped fresh mushrooms
2 T chopped parsley
2 T sliced celery
1 t chopped fresh dill weed
2 t salt
¼ t black pepper
2 lbs. sliced halibut
4 slices lemon
1 cup dry white wine

In a shallow casserole, spread carrots and dot with 3 tablespoons of butter. Spread onions and mushrooms over carrots. Sprinkle with parsley, celery, dill, 1 teaspoon salt and pepper. Place fish slices on vegetables and sprinkle with 1 teaspoon of salt. Place lemon slices on top and dot with 3 tablespoons butter. Pour wine over fish and cover tightly with foil. Bake in a 400° preheated oven for 20 minutes. Remove foil and bake for another 20 minutes.

An Italian specialty, quick and easty to prepare, clams in a sauce of butter, olive oil and garlic served over linguini pasta

WHITE CLAM SAUCE WITH LINGUINI

½ cup butter
4 T olive oil
2 garlic cloves, finely minced
2 cups clam juice
2 cups minced clams
½ cup chopped parsley
8-ounces linguini

Heat butter and oil; add garlic and cook until golden. Stir in clam juice and simmer uncovered for 10 minutes. Add clams and parsley. Season with salt and pepper to taste. Cook until thoroughly heated. Cook linguini in boiling salted water until tender and drain. Serve sauce over hot linguini.

Sweet and pungent Hawaiian shrimp in a sauce of pineapple chunks, green pepper and onions

HAWAIIAN SHRIMP

2½ cups pineapple chunks, with juice
4 T brown sugar
2 T cornstarch
½ t salt
¼ cup vinegar
1 T soy sauce
1 large green bell pepper, cut in ¼-inch strips
2 small onions, cut in rings
2 cups cooked and cleaned shrimp

Drain pineapple liquid into saucepan. Add brown sugar, cornstarch, salt, vinegar and soy sauce; mix thoroughly. Cook until slightly thickened, stirring constantly. Add green pepper, onions and pineapple chunks; cook for 2 to 3 minutes. Remove from heat; add shrimp and let stand for 10 minutes. Just before serving, bring to a boil, stirring constantly. Excellent served over hot rice.

A hearty cool summer meal, Swedish herring salad made with potatoes, beets and hard-boiled eggs

HERRING SALAD

4 T vinegar
¼ t black pepper
1 t chopped onion
2 salt herring fillets, cut in ¼-inch cubes
4 medium cold boiled potatoes, cut in ¼-inch cubes
4 medium cold boiled beets, cut in ¼-inch cubes
1 medium gherkin pickle, cut in ¼-inch cubes
1 medium apple, cut in ¼-inch cubes
2 hard-boiled eggs, separate yolk from white and mince
    separately
¼ cup minced parsley
Sour cream

Mix vinegar, black pepper and onion in a bowl. Add herring, potatoes, beets, pickle and apple. Mix carefully with two forks. Spoon salad into serving dish; press down so surface is even. Chill for 30 minutes. Decorate top of salad with stripes of egg yolk, parsley and egg white. Serve salad with sour cream.

The Greeks prepare this delicious lobster tail entree with a sauce of tomatoes and onions, topped with feta cheese

LOBSTER TAILS WITH FETA CHEESE

1 cup finely minced onion
4 T olive oil
1 garlic clove, finely minced
2 cups drained plum tomatoes, chopped
⅓ cup tomato sauce
¼ t oregano
¼ t sugar
⅛ t dry mustard
¼ t freshly ground black pepper
¼ cup finely minced parsley
8 small lobster tails, uncooked
3 T butter
¼ cup flour
¼ lb. feta cheese, thinly sliced

Sauté onion in olive oil without browning. Add garlic, tomatoes, tomato sauce, oregano, sugar, mustard, black pepper and parsley. Cook, uncovered, until sauce thickens, about 30 minutes. Shell the lobster, being careful to remove the meat in one piece. Heat the butter in a skillet. Lightly dust lobster tails with flour and quickly sauté in butter until firm, about two minutes. In a shallow glass baking dish place lobster and cover with the cooked tomato sauce. Top with feta cheese and bake in a 425° preheated oven until cheese melts, about 10 minutes.

A gourmet treat from Mexico, avocado halves heaped with crab in a delicious sauce

MEXICAN CRAB ACAPULCO

4 T butter
4 T flour
1⅔ cups milk
1¼ t salt
1 t Worcestershire sauce
Dash of cayenne pepper
2 T lemon juice
3 T dry sherry
⅓ cup grated sharp Cheddar cheese
2 cups cooked crabmeat
4 medium avocados
Toasted sesame seeds or toasted coconut

Melt butter in saucepan; blend in flour. Gradually blend in milk; cook, stirring constantly until thickened and smooth. Add ¾ teaspoon salt, Worcestershire sauce, cayenne, lemon juice, sherry and cheese; mix well. Add crabmeat and cook until just heated. Cut avocados in half; remove stones and skins. Place in a shallow baking dish; sprinkle with ½ teaspoon salt and heap with crab mixture. Top with sesame seeds or coconut. Bake in a 300° preheated oven for 15 minutes only, or until just warm.

Fiskesuppe, a simple and hearty Norwegian fish soup made with fish fillets, leeks, potatoes and garnished with dill

NORWEGIAN FISH SOUP

2 T butter
2 leeks, thinly sliced
4 medium potatoes, peeled and diced
½ cup diced celery
5 cups water
1 t salt
½ t black pepper
1 lb. fish fillets, cut in 1-inch squares
1 T chopped fresh dill weed

In a large heavy skillet melt butter; sauté leeks, potatoes and celery over low heat, about 5 minutes. Add water, salt and pepper. Bring to a boil and cook until vegetables are tender, about 10 to 15 minutes. Add fish and cook another 10 minutes. Taste for seasoning, add salt if necessary. Sprinkle with dill and serve immediately.

With the abundance of seafood from the Mediterranean, a favorite is an interesting combination of shrimps, clams and lobster tails

MEDITERRANEAN SEAFOOD

6 T olive oil
2 garlic cloves, finely minced
4 small lobster tails, cut through shell into 1-inch slices
12 large uncooked shrimp, shell split down the back and deveined
2 cups drained cooked plum tomatoes
¾ cup dry white wine
½ t oregano
1 bay leaf
1 t salt
¼ t freshly ground black pepper
12 cherrystone clams, scrubbed and washed
2 T finely minced parsley

In a large skillet heat olive oil and cook garlic for 1 minute. Add lobster and shrimp; cook for 2 minutes. Stir in tomatoes, wine, oregano, bay leaf, salt and pepper. Cook briskly for about 5 to 7 minutes. Add clams and cover skillet, cook 10 to 12 minutes, stirring occasionally, until the clams open. Remove from heat and sprinkle with parsley.

Here is a unique and unusual seafood salad from a Hong Kong hotel dining room combining crab, shrimp, pineapple, water chestnuts and pine nuts; with a superb dressing

PARADISE SEAFOOD SALAD

1 cup flaked crabmeat
1 cup cooked shrimp
2 cups diced fresh pineapple
¼ cup finely sliced green onion
2 T currants
3 T lime juice
1 cup diced celery
½ cup diced water chestnuts
4 T chutney
1 t curry powder
½ t salt
1 cup mayonnaise
½ cup sour cream
¼ cup shelled pine nuts
Lettuce leaves
Paprika

In a bowl combine crab, shrimp, pineapple, green onion, currants, lime juice, celery, water chestnuts, chutney, curry powder and salt. Toss gently, but thoroughly. Just before serving blend mayonnaise and sour cream; gently toss into salad. Line serving platter with lettuce leaves and spoon on salad mixture. Scatter pine nuts over top of salad and sprinkle with paprika.

Here is an Indonesian recipe offering an exotic, highly seasoned combination of prawns and green beans

PRAWN AND GREEN BEAN CURRY

2 T oil
2 cups chopped onion
2 garlic cloves, finely minced
1 t grated fresh gingerroot
⅛ t cayenne
1 bay leaf
1 T water
½ t coriander
16 prawns, shelled and deveined
1 cup cooked cut green beans
2 T vinegar
½ t salt

In a large skillet heat oil; add onion, garlic, ginger root, cayenne and bay leaf. Cook and stir for about 5 minutes. Add water and coriander; cook another 5 minutes. Add uncooked prawns, green beans, vinegar and salt. Cook and stir quickly until prawns are just tender, about 5 minutes. Remove bay leaf and serve immediately. Excellent served with rice.

Italian Shrimp Marinara, shrimps in a sauce of tomatoes, onion, garlic and wine

SHRIMP MARINARA

2 garlic cloves, cut in half
1 medium onion, finely chopped
5 T olive oil
2 lbs. uncooked shrimp, shelled and deveined
3½ cups cooked plum tomatoes
1 T chopped parsley
¾ t salt
½ t freshly ground black pepper
½ cup dry sherry

Sauté garlic and onion in olive oil for about 5 minutes; remove garlic. Add shrimp, cover and cook 5 minutes or until shrimp turn pink. Add tomatoes, parsley, salt and pepper; simmer for 5 minutes. Add sherry; continue cooking for another 10 minutes.

Joppes Räksallad, a delicious Danish salad luncheon of shrimp, mushrooms, tomatoes and asparagus

SHRIMP SALAD

2 cups cooked shrimp
2½ cups sliced fresh mushrooms
2 medium tomatoes, cut in wedges
1 cup cooked asparagus spears
2 T oil
2 t vinegar
½ t salt
¼ t chopped dill weed
Crisp lettuce leaves
2 hard-boiled eggs, cut in wedges

In a bowl combine shrimp, mushrooms, tomatoes and asparagus. Combine oil, vinegar, salt and dill; mix thoroughly; pour over shrimp mixture and gently toss. Arrange on lettuce leaves; garnish with egg wedges.

A beautifully delicate salmon custard offered as a tasty London specialty

SALMON CUSTARD

2 eggs, slightly beaten
1 cup evaporated milk
½ t salt
¼ t black pepper
2 cups cooked salmon, flaked
¼ t paprika

Combine eggs, milk, salt and pepper. Add salmon and pour into greased baking dish. Sprinkle with paprika. Place baking dish in pan of hot water. Bake in a 350° preheated oven for 50 minutes or until firm.

In Mozambique, Africa, they prepare Peixe à Lumbo, a fish and shrimp delight stewed in a spicy sauce of tomatoes, peppers and coconut milk

FISH AND SHRIMP STEW

8 small sea bass or red snapper steaks, 1-inch thick
1½ t salt
3 T olive oil
1½ cups finely chopped onion
2 medium green bell peppers, cut in 1-inch pieces
1 hot yellow chili pepper, finely minced
2 medium tomatoes, finely chopped
1 T finely minced fresh coriander
1 lb. uncooked shrimp, shell and devein
½ cup coconut milk, or ¼ cup coconut and ½ cup hot water mixed in blender

Season fish steaks with ½ teaspoon of salt and set aside. In a large skillet heat olive oil, add onion, bell pepper and chili pepper. Stirring frequently, sauté for 5 minutes or until soft. Add tomatoes; cook, stirring frequently, until most of the liquid in the pan evaporates and the mixture is thick. Remove from heat; add coriander, 1 teaspoon of salt and taste for seasoning. Arrange 4 fish steaks in a heavy saucepan in one layer. Scatter half of the shrimp over and around fish; spoon half of vegetable mixture over. Add remaining steaks and sprinkle with shrimp; cover with remaining vegetables. Pour in the coconut milk and bring to a simmer over moderate heat. Reduce heat and cook, partially covered, until shrimp are firm and pink, about 12 minutes. Delicious served with rice.

A California favorite, green peppers stuffed with shrimp and mushrooms, a la Laguna Beach

PEPPERS STUFFED WITH SHRIMP

4 large green bell peppers
¼ t minced onion
1 T butter
½ cup chopped fresh mushrooms
1 small tomato, finely chopped
2 cups cooked shrimp
1 t salt
1 t minced parsley
¼ cup buttered bread crumbs

Cut slice from stem end of peppers, remove seeds and wash thoroughly. Parboil peppers for 5 minutes. Chop end slices of peppers and cook with onion in butter until tender. Add mushrooms and tomato; cook another 10 minutes. Add shrimp, salt and parsley. Fill peppers with mixture; sprinkle with bread crumbs and place in baking dish. Bake in a 350° preheated oven for 30 minutes.

Besugo al Horno, is red snapper baked with potatoes, Spanish style

RED SNAPPER BAKED WITH POTATOES

2 2-lb. whole red snappers
1 lemon, cut into 6 wedges
1½ t salt
¾ cup fine soft bread crumbs
1 t finely chopped garlic
2 T finely chopped parsley
2 T paprika
3 medium potatoes, peeled and cut in ¼-inch slices
¼ t freshly ground black pepper

1 cup water
6 T olive oil

With a sharp knife, score each fish by making three crosswise parallel cuts about ¼ inch deep and 2 inches long. Insert a wedge of lemon, skin side up in each cut. Sprinkle fish with 1 teaspoon salt. In a bowl combine bread crumbs, garlic, parsley and paprika; mix thoroughly. Spread potato slices evenly on the bottom of a baking dish. Sprinkle with ½ teaspoon salt and pepper. Place fish side by side on top of potatoes. Pour water down the side of the baking dish; spoon olive oil over fish. Sprinkle fish evenly with bread crumb mixture. Bake in a 350° preheated oven for 30 minutes or until fish feels firm and potatoes are done.

Sayur Asem, a tempting Indonesian dish of tender crisp celery, shrimp and spices served over rice

SHRIMP AND CELERY

2 T chopped onion
2 garlic cloves, chopped
½ t coarse-ground hot red pepper
½ t salt
1 t cardamom seeds
1½ cups water
1 medium-sized bunch of celery, cleaned and cut crosswise in ¾-inch slices
1½ cups shelled, deveined, chopped raw shrimp
2 T lemon juice
2 cups hot cooked rice

In a mortar with pestle (or blender), combine and crush; onion, garlic, red pepper, salt and cardamom. Add water and blend. In a saucepan bring spice and water mixture to a boil; add celery, simmer 5 minutes. Add shrimp and lemon juice, continue to simmer for another 8 to 10 minutes. Serve over rice.

The French have a style of sautéing trout and serving with a simple but delicate wine and lemon sauce

SAUTÉED TROUT IN WINE SAUCE

4 trout, about 1 lb. each
1 t salt
¼ t black pepper
½ cup flour
¼ cup corn meal
5 T butter
6 T oil
2 T chopped parsley
1 lemon, sliced

Season trout with salt and pepper. Mix flour and cornmeal together; roll trout in mixture until well coated. In a heavy skillet heat butter and oil. Over medium heat, sauté trout until golden brown, about 5 to 7 minutes on each side. Place fish on a heated platter and quickly prepare wine sauce. Pour wine sauce over trout and sprinkle with parsley. Garnish with lemon slices.

Wine Sauce:

1 T butter
1 T flour
½ cup dry white wine
½ cup lemon juice

In a small saucepan, heat butter and stir in flour. Gradually add wine; stirring constantly, bring to a boil. Add lemon juice and continue cooking until slightly thickened.

Zucchini and dill give this tuna casserole a wonderful Scandinavian flavor

ZUCCHINI-TUNA CASSEROLE

5 T butter
1½ cups coarsely shredded fresh zucchini
1 cup sliced celery
½ cup chopped onion
4 T flour
2 cups milk
¾ cup grated Parmesan cheese
¼ cup chopped parsley
1¼ t salt
1 t chopped dill weed
3 cups cooked spiral macaroni
2 cups tuna, drained of oil
1 cup fresh bread crumbs
Paprika

In a saucepan melt 3 tablespoons butter and sauté zucchini, celery and onion for a few minutes. Stir in flour and cook slowly, stirring constantly, for 2 minutes. Remove from heat; blend in milk, ½ cup grated cheese, parsley, salt and dill weed. Return to heat; cook, stirring constantly, until it comes to a boil and thickens. Add macaroni and tuna; mix well. Pour mixture into a buttered casserole. Combine bread crumbs, ¼ cup cheese and 2 tablespoons butter. Top casserole with crumb mixture and lightly sprinkle with paprika. Bake in a 325° preheated oven for 35 minutes.

A Swedish recipe of fish and rice rolled in leaves of cabbage and served with tangy lemon-egg sauce

STUFFED CABBAGE ROLLS

1 medium-sized green cabbage
2 small onions, chopped
4 T butter
1 lb. skinned and boned fish, coarsely chopped
2 T chopped parsley
3 T grated Parmesan cheese
½ cup cooked rice
2 eggs, slightly beaten
1 t salt
¼ t cayenne pepper
¼ t cinnamon
3 T tomato paste dissolved in 2 cups water
1 cup dry white wine
1 egg yolk
3 T lemon juice
Freshly ground black pepper

Plunge cabbage in boiling water for 5 minutes. Drain, detach leaves, paring down heavier ribs. Sauté onions in 1 tablespoon butter until transparent. In a bowl, combine sautéed onions, fish, parsley, cheese, rice, eggs, salt, cayenne pepper and cinnamon; mix well. Onto each cabbage leaf place 3 heaping spoons of fish mixture and roll into a cylinder shape. Heat 3 tablespoons butter in a large heavy skillet and quickly brown cabbage rolls. Combine tomato paste-water mixture and wine; pour over rolls. Lay a plate over cabbage rolls (to keep them from breaking); cook slowly for 45 minutes. Gently lift out rolls and put on a hot serving dish. Mix egg yolk and lemon juice in a bowl and stir in a little hot liquid from skillet. Pour back into skillet. Stirring constantly, heat until hot but not boiling. Taste for seasoning and pour over cabbage rolls. Sprinkle with a little freshly ground black pepper.

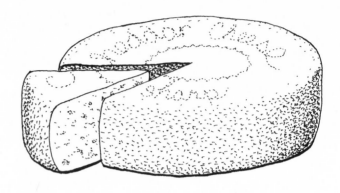

Shrimp baked on a bed of spinach, covered with sauce and Cheddar cheese, a lovely taste sensation from the Virgin Islands

SHRIMP AND SPINACH WITH CHEDDAR CHEESE

4 cups cooked chopped spinach
3 cups cooked cleaned shrimp
4 T butter
4 T flour
1½ cups milk
½ cup dry white wine
½ cup thinly sliced green onions
1 t salt
½ t freshly ground black pepper
1 T paprika
1 cup shredded Cheddar cheese

In a shallow casserole spread spinach and top with shrimp. In a saucepan, melt butter and stir in flour; gradually add milk and wine. Add green onions; cook, stirring constantly over low heat until sauce bubbles and thickens, about 5 minutes. Add salt, pepper and paprika; pour over shrimp. Sprinkle top with Cheddar cheese; bake in a 350° preheated oven for 35 minutes, or until bubbly.

A Chinese favorite, small omelets made with eggs, bean sprouts, water chestnuts, mushrooms and shrimp

SHRIMP FOO YONG

1 cup chopped cooked shrimp
1⅓ cup bean sprouts, rinsed and drained
3 T finely chopped water chestnuts
1½ T chopped green onion
4 fresh mushrooms, chopped
6 eggs
3 T salad oil

Combine shrimp, bean sprouts, water chestnuts, green onion and mushrooms. Add eggs and mix thoroughly. Brush griddle or skillet with oil. Drop about ⅓ cup of egg mixture onto hot griddle. Cook over medium heat till lightly browned, turn and brown other side. Keep warm while frying remaining mixture. These may be served plain or with Foo Yong Sauce.

Foo Yong Sauce:

1 T cornstarch
¼ t salt
2 T soy sauce
1 cup chicken broth

In a small saucepan, blend cornstarch and salt. Gradually stir in soy sauce. Add chicken broth; cook and stir till mixture thickens and bubbles.

An easy to prepare luncheon salad is Italian Insalata di Riso, made with rice, artichoke hearts, eggs and tuna

TUNA AND RICE SALAD

4 T olive oil
4 T lemon juice
2 T chopped parsley
1 t dried basil
1 t salt
½ t freshly ground black pepper
3 cups cooked rice, tender but firm
1 cup tuna, drained of oil
2 T capers
1 cup coarsely chopped marinated artichoke hearts
2 hard-boiled eggs, sliced

In a salad bowl mix olive oil, lemon juice, parsley, basil, salt and black pepper. Add rice and gently toss together. Add tuna, capers, artichokes; carefully mixing with rice. Taste for seasoning and decorate top with egg slices. Let stand at room temperature for 15 minutes and serve.

A California coast taste sensation; shrimp, cream, blue cheese and tomato baked in a surprise foil packet

SHRIMP AND TOMATO SURPRISES

6 ounces cream cheese
½ cup crumbled blue cheese
2 T minced black olives
2 pimentos, finely chopped
1 T grated onion
⅛ t black pepper
2 large tomatoes, halved
2 cups cooked shrimp
4 lemon slices

Mash cream and blue cheese to a paste. Add olives, pimentos, onion and pepper. Whip mixture until fluffy. Place each tomato half on a square of aluminum foil. Sprinkle tomatoes with salt and pepper if desired. Arrange shrimp on tomato halves. Spoon cheese mixture on shrimp. Top each with a lemon slice. Bring foil up around food to form a bag; close tightly. Place on a baking sheet; cook in a 400° preheated oven for 20 minutes. minutes.

French Salmon pâté, a most enjoyable cool lunch on a warm summer day

SALMON PÂTÉ

1 T unflavored gelatin
1 cup half and half
1 cup cooked salmon
2 t onion powder
1 t lemon juice
½ t black pepper
½ t salt
½ t garlic powder
1 cup heavy cream, whipped
8 parsley sprigs

Sprinkle gelatin onto ½ cup half and half in a small saucepan, to soften. Place over low heat, stirring constantly, until dissolved. Put salmon, ½ cup half and half, onion powder, lemon juice, pepper, salt and garlic powder in blender; puree until smooth. Add dissolved gelatin and blend for 1 minute. Remove salmon mixture from blender and fold in whipped cream. Spoon mixture into a suitable mold or loaf pan. Chill in refrigerator for 3 hours or until firm. Unmold onto serving platter and garnish with parsley sprigs.

Mushrooms stuffed with green chilies and onion Mexican style; excellent served as an appetizer.

SHRIMP-STUFFED MUSHROOMS

12 large mushrooms
2 T thinly sliced green onion
2 T finely chopped green chili pepper
4 T butter
½ cup small cooked shrimp
1 T dry sherry
1 egg yolk

Remove and chop stems of mushrooms. In a skillet, sauté stems, onion and chilies in 2 tablespoons butter until soft. Stir in shrimp and sherry. Beat egg yolk and stir in a little hot liquid from vegetables. Add egg yolk to vegetables; cook and stir for 1 minute. Remove from heat. Spoon filling into mushroom caps. In the skillet, melt 2 tablespoons butter. Carefully place filled mushrooms in skillet. Cover and cook until mushrooms are tender, about 3 to 4 minutes. Lovely served in small shells with oyster forks.

Camarones Rancheros is a spicy, hot Mexican creation of shrimp and green chilies

SHRIMP AND CHILIES

1 garlic clove, minced
½ medium onion, sliced
2 jalapeno or hot yellow chili peppers, sliced
1 T chopped fresh cilantro
2 T butter
2 medium tomatoes, diced
6 fresh long green chilies, chopped
¼ t sugar
½ t salt
6 T oil
2 dozen uncooked large shrimp, peeled, deveined and
    butterflied

Sauté garlic, onion, jalapeno chilies and cilantro in butter over low heat until onion is tender. Add tomato, green chilies, sugar, and salt; cook 3 minutes. In a large skillet heat oil and sauté shrimp until pink, about 5 minutes. Add chilie sauce and cook 1 minute longer. Traditionally served with rice.

Mexican Ceviche may be served as a cool main dish, salad or appetizer; white fish marinated in lime juice, combined with tomatoes, onions and cilantro

CEVICHE

1 lb. lean white fish, cut in 1-inch squares
⅔ cup lime juice
2 medium tomatoes, chopped
⅓ cup finely minced onion
1 T coarsely chopped, fresh cilantro
½ t dried oregano
½ fresh hot yellow chili, finely minced
2 T oil
1 T dry white wine
2 t white vinegar
¾ t salt

In a glass bowl place fish and lime juice; mix with a wooden spoon. Let stand until fish becomes opaque, stirring occasionally. If desired, marinate fish overnight in refrigerator. Place fish in a strainer and rinse thoroughly with cold water; squeeze out excess moisture. Combine fish, tomatoes, onion, cilantro, oregano and chili. Add oil, wine, vinegar and salt; mix thoroughly. Cover and chill several hours before serving.

The Greeks prepare Garides me Saltsa; shrimp in a tomato, wine and Feta cheese sauce, traditionally accompanied with crusty loaves of bread and a glass of Retsina wine

SHRIMP IN TOMATO, WINE AND FETA CHEESE SAUCE

1½ lbs. medium-sized raw shrimp
5 T olive oil
¼ cup finely chopped onion
4 large ripe tomatoes, peeled and chopped
½ cup dry white wine
2 T finely chopped parsley
½ t crumbled oregano
1 t salt
½ t freshly ground black pepper
⅓ cup Feta cheese cut in ¼-inch cubes

Shell and devein shrimp; leaving last shell segment and tail attached. Wash and drain well. In a heavy skillet or shallow casserole, heat olive oil over moderate heat. Add onions and stirring frequently, cook for 5 minutes or until soft, but not browned. Stir in tomatoes, wine, 1 tablespoon parsley, oregano, salt and pepper. Bring to a boil and cook briskly, uncovered, until mixture thickens. Add shrimp and cook 5 minutes longer. When shrimp is pink and firm to the touch, stir in cheese. Top with remaining parsley and serve directly from skillet or casserole.

Italians enjoy a delightful hot shrimp appetizer served from a chafing dish or as a main course served over rice

SCAMPI

4 T butter
1 garlic clove, finely minced
2 T minced parsley
½ cup dry white wine
2½ cups cooked shrimp

Melt butter in skillet or chafing dish. Add garlic, parsley and wine. Heat to simmering; add shrimp and cook over low heat until heated through, about 5 minutes.

This is an Australian recipe for fish fillets baked on a colorful bed of spinach, tomatoes and onions

BAKED FISH WITH SPINACH

2 medium onions, thinly sliced
2 T oil
4 medium tomatoes, peeled and chopped
Salt to taste
¼ t black pepper
¼ t thyme
1 bay leaf
4 fish fillets, about ½ lb. each
1 T flour
2 T butter
1 bunch spinach, cooked and finely chopped
3 T cream or milk
Dash of nutmeg

Sauté onions in 1 tablespoon of oil. Add tomatoes, salt, pepper, thyme and bay leaf; cover and simmer 20 minutes. Remove lid, and cook till liquid is evaporated. Spoon into baking dish. Sprinkle fish with salt and dip in flour. In a skillet, heat butter and 1 tablespoon oil; quickly brown fish on both sides and place on mixture in baking dish. In a bowl combine spinach, cream, nutmeg, salt and pepper to taste; spoon around fish. Cover with foil and bake in a 350° preheated oven for 15 minutes; remove foil and brown quickly under broiler.

The Hungarians enjoy an easily prepared casserole of fish fillets, potatoes and mushrooms topped with wine and sour cream

BAKED FISH AND POTATOES

4 medium potatoes, cooked, peeled and thinly sliced
2 T butter
1 cup sour cream
1 cup sliced mushrooms
⅔ cup dry white wine
1 t salt
¼ t black pepper
2 lbs. fish fillets
2 T chopped parsley or fresh dill weed

In a buttered baking dish, arrange potato slices and dot with butter. Spread with ½-cup sour cream. Add layer of mushroom slices. Sprinkle with wine, salt and pepper. Over this arrange fish fillets. Top with remaining sour cream and sprinkle with parsley or dill weed. Bake in a 350° preheated oven until fish is cooked, about 30 minutes.

Excellent for a summer luncheon, West African avocado stuffed with smoked fish

AVOCADO STUFFED WITH SMOKED FISH

4 hard-boiled eggs
¼ cup milk
¼ t sugar
½ t salt
4 T strained lime juice
5 T vegetable oil
2 T olive oil
1 cup smoked fish skinned, boned and finely flaked
2 large ripe avocados
lettuce leaves
1 medium red pimento or green bell pepper cut in ¼-inch strips

In a deep bowl, with a fork mash egg yolks and milk into a smooth paste. Add sugar, salt and 1 tablespoon of lime juice. Beat in vegetable oil 1 tablespoon at a time. Add olive oil in the same manner. Stir in remaining lime juice; taste for seasoning. Mince egg whites with fish, add to dressing and toss. Just before serving, cut avocados in half and remove stones; arrange on a bed of lettuce leaves. Spoon mixture into avocado halves, decorate with pepper strips.

Yugoslavians prepare their baked fish in a distinctive manner, served with a yogurt sauce

BAKED FISH WITH YOGURT SAUCE

3 medium onions, thinly sliced
2 garlic cloves, finely minced
4 T olive oil
1 T paprika
3 T tomato paste
3 T chopped parsley
1 t salt
¼ t black pepper
1 cup dry white wine
1 4 lb. whole, firm white fish, dressed

Sauté onions and garlic in olive oil until soft; add paprika and cook 1 minute. Stir in tomato paste, parsley, salt, pepper, and wine. Pour mixture over fish arranged in a baking dish. Bake in a 350° preheated oven for about 45 minutes, baste occasionally with pan juices. Remove fish carefully to a warm platter, serve with yogurt sauce.

Yogurt Sauce

Pan juices from baked fish
2 T flour
1 cup plain yogurt

Stir flour into pan juices, add yogurt and mix well. Cook over low heat, stirring constantly for 5 minutes.

chicken

The ways of preparing chicken seem almost unending, subject only to the cook's creative imagination. The Chinese cooked chicken as early as 1400 B.C. Since the time of the earliest nomads, chickens have been man's most constant edible traveling food resource. Chickens sailed with the early English, Dutch, Spanish and Portuguese explorers. The Spanish brought the first chickens to the Americas in the 16th Century, and more arrived with the Pilgrims. Chicken is a favorite dish everywhere, each country seems to have a national chicken dish for which it is justly famous. Each uses its own flavoring specialty, such as wine in France; curries in India; mole sauce in Mexico; tomato sauce in Italy; paprika in Hungary. Nutritionally an excellent source of high quality protein, chicken also contains a low amount of saturated fats. In fact, one pound of boned and skinned broiled chicken contains approximately 460 calories, fairly low compared to red meat. The gentle flavor and texture of chicken make it adaptable to many interesting dishes. The recipes in this chapter will provide you an opportunity to enjoy unique and varied favorites from around the world.

Buying Chicken

The fresh broiler-fryer is an all-purpose tender chicken weighing from 1½-3½ pounds, whole, halved, quartered or cut up. Chicken parts, breasts, thighs, legs, etc. may also be purchased. The number of servings from a chicken varies somewhat with the preparation and method of cooking. Generally, a 3-pound broiler-fryer will serve four. A 3-pound broiler-fryer yields about 2½-cups diced cooked chicken.

Storing Chicken

Remove the store wrapper from uncooked fresh chicken, rinse, drain and pat dry. Wrap chicken loosely and store in refrigerator until ready to cook. For maximum quality, use as soon as convenient; fresh chicken may be kept refrigerated 1-3 days. Frozen chicken must be kept frozen until ready to use, and once thawed must not be refrozen. For best results, frozen chicken should be defrosted overnight in the refrigerator, or in a microwave oven just before cooking. Cooked chicken should be served promptly after cooking. Immediately after the meal, refrigerate leftovers in covered containers. Left-over portions may be kept for 2-3 days for maximum quality and flavor.

How to Make Chicken Broth

When in a hurry broth may be made with chicken bouillon and hot water. When more time allows chicken broth is made with 4-pounds chicken parts (backs, necks, wings, etc.), 12 cups water, 1 sliced onion, 1 sliced carrot, 1 bay leaf, 2 sprigs parsley and 2 teaspoons salt. Combine all ingredients and simmer for 2 hours. Strain broth, cool, pour into 1-cup containers and freeze for later use.

Chicken

Bombay chicken of India combines chicken, rice, raisins, coconut and peanuts into a delicious casserole

BOMBAY CHICKEN

1 2½ lb. chicken, cut up
5 T flour
1 t paprika
1 t salt
4 T butter
1 medium onion, thinly sliced
3½ cups chicken broth
1 cup uncooked long-grain rice
½ yellow raisins
½ cup flaked coconut
¼ cup coarsely chopped roasted peanuts
1 t curry powder

Coat chicken with mixture of flour, paprika and salt. In a skillet, brown chicken in butter. Remove chicken; cook onion in remaining butter till tender but not brown. Add chicken broth and bring to a boil. Add rice, raisins, coconut, peanuts and curry powder. Taste for seasoning. Turn rice mixture into a 12×7×2-inch baking dish. Top with chicken. Bake covered in a 350° preheated oven until rice is cooked and chicken is tender, about 1½ hours.

Tarnegolet Bemizt Hadarim is an easy to prepare, yet exotically flavored, Israeli oven baked chicken with kumquats and orange juice

BAKED CHICKEN WITH KUMQUATS

1 2½ lb. chicken, cut up
1 t salt
1 cup orange juice
2 T lemon juice
4 T honey
1 T minced hot chili pepper
12 preserved kumquats
1 medium orange, sliced

Sprinkle chicken with salt; arrange in a baking dish in one layer. Mix orange juice, lemon juice, honey and chili pepper together; pour over chicken pieces, turning until all are well moistened. Bake uncovered in a 375° preheated oven for 15 minutes; turn, add kumquats and baste chicken with pan juices. Bake for another 30 minutes, basting occasionally, until leg or thigh shows no resistance when pierced with a fork. To serve, arrange chicken and kumquats on a heated platter, pour the pan juices over and garnish with orange slices.

Chicken and dark sweet cherries combine in a spectacular flaming entree suitable for a dinner party, turn down the lights before serving to guests for a dramatic effect

CHERRY CHICKEN JUBILEE

6 T flour
1 t salt
¼ t garlic powder
⅛ t black pepper
4 small whole chicken breasts, skinned, boned and halved
4 T butter
1½ cups dry white wine
1½ cups drained pitted dark sweet cherries (reserve liquid for sauce)
¼ cup Brandy

Mix together flour, salt, garlic powder and pepper in a bag. Add chicken pieces, one at a time and shake to coat thoroughly. Heat butter in a large skillet, add chicken and brown on all sides. Remove chicken from skillet and arrange in a 8×8-inch baking dish; pour wine over and cover with foil. Bake in a 350° preheated oven for 25 minutes. Add cherries to chicken and bake uncovered for another 20 minutes. Arrange chicken in a heated chafing dish. Pour 1 cup of prepared sauce over chicken, top with warm brandy and ignite.

Sauce:

wine liquid from cooked chicken
2 T flour
About ½ cup drained liquid from cherries

Pour wine liquid from baking dish into a small saucepan. Dissolve flour in cherry liquid, add to saucepan; bring to a boil, stirring constantly, until sauce thickens.

Chicken Sevillano, a robustly flavored Spanish way of preparing chicken with artichoke hearts in a delicious sauce

ARTICHOKE HEARTS AND CHICKEN

3 T olive oil
3 T butter
1 garlic clove, finely minced
1 3 lb. chicken, cut up
1 t salt
¼ t black pepper
1 leek, thinly sliced
1 carrot, diced
1 medium onion, chopped
1 cup chopped mushrooms
1 cup cooked artichoke hearts, cut in halves
¾ cup sliced pimento-stuffed green olives
1 cup dry red wine
½ bay leaf
⅛ t thyme
Chicken broth as needed

In a large frying pan, heat olive oil, butter and garlic. Sprinkle chicken with salt and pepper; sauté on both sides until browned; remove. Add leek, carrot, onion and mushrooms to the pan; cook, stirring constantly until vegetables are browned and soft. Return chicken to pan along with artichoke hearts, ½ cup olives, wine, bay leaf and thyme. Cover and simmer slowly until chicken is tender, about 30 minutes. Remove chicken and artichokes to a serving platter and keep warm. Press remaining mixture in pan through a seive or beat in a blender. Return mixture to pan, thin to sauce consistency with chicken broth. Taste for seasoning. Pour sauce over chicken and garnish with remaining ¼ cup sliced olives. Serve at once.

Chicken Tocană, is a Romanian stew deliciously flavored with black olives, sour cream and wine

CHICKEN AND OLIVE STEW

1 3 lb. chicken, cut up
3 T olive oil
1 large onion, thinly sliced
1 garlic clove, finely minced
1 t salt
¼ t freshly ground black pepper
2 cups dry white wine
1 cup sliced pitted black olives
½ cup chopped parsley
½ cup sour cream

In a large frying pan brown chicken in olive oil. Add onions and garlic; sauté with chicken for 5 minutes. Sprinkle with salt and pepper, add wine, cover and cook slowly for about 1 hour. Add olives, parsley and sour cream. Simmer another 5 minutes and taste for seasoning.

Hawaiian brochette of chicken and pineapple broiled with an orange glaze

CHICKEN AND PINEAPPLE BROCHETTE

4 T melted butter
⅔ cup orange juice
1 t dry mustard
1½ t grated orange rind
⅓ cup pineapple juice
1 T sautern wine
2 large whole chicken breasts, boned and cut into
    bite-sized pieces
2 cups pineapple cubes or chunks

Combine melted butter, orange juice, dry mustard, grated orange rind, pineapple juice and wine. Mix thoroughly and marinate chicken in the mixture for several hours. On skewers, alternate chicken and pineapple pieces. Broil, about 5 inches from the heat source for about 8 minutes, occasionally basting with the marinade. Turn and cook for another 5 minutes. Excellent served with brown or wild rice.

Chicken and okra are combined in a well-seasoned Yugoslavian stew, cooked slowly to blend the flavors and seasonings

CHICKEN AND OKRA STEW

3 T butter
1 3 lb. chicken, cut up
1 t salt
½ t freshly ground black pepper
2 medium onions, sliced
2 cups uncooked sliced okra
1 cup chopped green bell pepper
⅛ t cayenne pepper
1 cup chicken broth
3 T tomato paste
3 T chopped parsley

In a skillet heat butter and sauté chicken on both sides until golden. As pieces are browned, place in a heavy casserole. Season with salt and black pepper. Sauté onions in drippings and spoon over chicken. Top with okra and green peppers. In a saucepan combine cayenne, chicken broth and tomato paste. Bring to a boil and pour over chicken and vegetables. Cover and cook over a very low flame until chicken is tender, about 40 minutes. Taste for seasoning; sprinkle with parsley just before serving.

La Tze Chi is a popular dish in the provincial region of Southern China, chicken with hot peppers served over rice

CHICKEN AND HOT PEPPERS

2 large whole chicken breasts
4 T peanut or salad oil
12 large long green chili peppers, deveined and cut in
    1-inch squares
1 t salt
2 t sugar
1½ t finely chopped candied ginger
1 garlic clove, finely minced
2½ cups chicken broth
1 T cornstarch
2 cups hot cooked rice

Place chicken breasts in pan, cover with water and boil for 25 minutes. Remove chicken, cool; remove skin and bones, cut into small pieces. Measure broth, add water to make 2½ cups. In a large skillet or wok, heat oil and sauté peppers for 3 minutes. Add chicken, salt, sugar, ginger, garlic and chicken broth, cover and cook for about 5 minutes at a boil. Remove a few spoonfulls of sauce and mix with cornstarch to make a paste. Add to chicken and cook stirring constantly, 2 minutes longer. Taste for seasoning and serve immediately over hot cooked rice.

Italians enjoy Cioppino; here is one made with chicken and shrimp simmered in wine, tomato sauce and herbs

CHICKEN AND SHRIMP CIOPPINO

1 2½ lb. chicken, cut up
4 T butter
2 cups tomato sauce
½ cup claret wine
¾ cup finely chopped onion
1 garlic clove, finely minced
3 T minced parsley
1 t basil
1 bay leaf, crushed
1 t salt
½ t freshly ground black pepper
1 lb. raw shrimp, shelled and deveined

In a large frying pan, brown chicken slowly in butter. Add tomato sauce, wine, onion, garlic, parsley, basil, bay leaf, salt and pepper. Cover and simmer till chicken is tender, about 30 minutes. Add shrimp, being sure to immerse in sauce. Cover and continue cooking until shrimp is done, about 10 minutes. Serve in warm soup plates. Traditionally served with warm crusty Italian bread.

Hawaiians prepare chicken with pineapple and tomato sauce, seasoned with ginger

CHICKEN OAHU

1 3 lb. chicken, cut up
4 T flour
4 T butter
2 cups pineapple chunks
½ cup pineapple juice
2 T brown sugar
1 t ginger
¾ t salt
1 cup tomato sauce
¾ cup chicken broth

Coat chicken with flour; brown slowly in butter. Mix pineapple, pineapple juice, sugar, ginger and salt; add to chicken. Stir in tomato sauce and chicken broth; simmer, covered, for 20 minutes. Uncover and cook for another 25 minutes.

For a festive occasion, a gourmet treat; Cannelloni Capriccio, a delicate Italian pasta filled with chicken, spinach and mushrooms, covered with a creamy sauce

CHICKEN CANNELLONI

Pasta:

2 cups flour
2 eggs
1½ T water
¾ t salt

In a bowl, combine all ingredients and knead until it makes a smooth pasta dough. On board, roll dough paper-thin. Cut into 3-inch squares. Cook 6 at a time in 4 quarts boiling water for 5 minutes. Remove with slotted spoon and drain flat.

Filling:

1 cup chopped mushrooms
2 T butter
2½ cups diced cooked chicken
½ cup cooked spinach, well-drained
⅓ cup grated Parmesan cheese
1 whole egg and 1 egg yolk
¼ t salt

Sauté mushrooms in butter for 5 minutes. Finely mince or put through coarse grinder, chicken, spinach and mushrooms. Mix thoroughly with cheese, eggs and salt.

Sauce:

1 T flour
¼ cup melted butter
1½ cups milk
¼ t salt
⅛ t black pepper
⅛ t nutmeg

4 T grated Parmesan cheese
1 egg yolk

In a saucepan, blend flour in melted butter and cook 1 minute. Gradually add milk, stirring constantly until smooth. Take off heat and stir in salt, pepper, nutmeg, 2 tablespoons cheese and egg yolk; mix thoroughly. Place equal amounts of filling on cooked pasta squares and roll up. In a large glass baking dish place rolls in a single layer. Cover with sauce, sprinkle with 2 tablespoons cheese, bake in a 375° preheated oven for 15 minutes.

Chicken in a sauce of tomatoes, mushrooms, green peppers and herbs, an Italian favorite with an excellent sauce for dunking hot crusty bread

CHICKEN CACCIATORE

1 3 lb. chicken, cut up
4 T olive oil
2 garlic cloves, finely minced
1 t salt
¼ t black pepper
¼ t cayenne pepper
½ t crumbled oregano
½ t basil
3½ cups cooked tomatoes
1 large green bell pepper, cut in strips ½-inch wide
2 cups whole small mushrooms
¼ cup dry white wine
¼ cup minced parsley

In a large heavy skillet, brown chicken in olive oil until golden. Add garlic, salt, pepper, cayenne, oregano, basil, tomatoes, green pepper and mushrooms. Cover and simmer slowly until tender, about 45 minutes. Add wine and taste for seasoning. Cook 10 minutes longer. Sprinkle with parsley.

An easy to prepare but sensational Laguna Beach, California, recipe of chicken and almonds baked in a cream sauce

CHICKEN AND ALMONDS BAKED IN CREAM

1 3 lb. chicken, cut up
6 T flour
6 T melted butter
1 t celery salt
1 t paprika
1 t salt
½ t curry powder
½ t freshly ground black pepper
1 cup whole button mushrooms
¾ cup sliced almonds
1½ cups half and half
½ cup sour cream
3 T fine bread crumbs blended with 1 T melted butter

Coat chicken pieces with flour. Blend into melted butter, celery salt, paprika, salt, curry powder and black pepper. Roll chicken pieces in seasoned butter, coating on all sides. Arrange chicken in a single layer in baking dish; add mushrooms and sprinkle evenly with almonds. Pour half and half between pieces. Cover and bake in a 350° preheated oven for 45 minutes. Uncover and spoon about ½ cup of the sauce into sour cream and mix together. Pour evenly over chicken. Top with buttered bread crumbs. Bake uncovered for another 15 minutes.

Italian Chicken Calabrian, delicious and exotic; chicken baked with wine, figs and orange slices

CHICKEN WITH FIGS AND ORANGES

1 3 lb. chicken, quartered
2 T olive oil
½ t dried oregano, crumbled
2 t minced parsley
1 garlic clove, finely minced
1 t salt
1 cup dry white wine
2 T lemon juice
8 fresh or cooked Kadota figs
1 medium orange, sliced ¼-inch thick
¼ cup dry sherry
Parsley sprigs

Brush chicken with olive oil and place in shallow baking pan, skin side up; sprinkle with oregano, minced parsley, garlic and salt. Bake uncovered in a 400° preheated oven until golden brown, about 25 minutes; baste often during cooking with mixture of white wine and lemon juice. Prick figs with fork and marinate with orange slices in sherry. Turn chicken; baste and cook another 20 minutes. Add figs and orange slices, continue cooking, basting with remaining sherry marinade until golden, about 10 minutes. Place chicken sections on a large platter and garnish attractively with figs, orange slices and sprigs of fresh parsley.

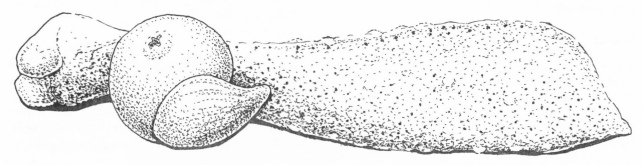

Pollo a la Pepitoria, a Spanish recipe prepared with wine and covered with a subtle almond sauce

CHICKEN WITH ALMOND SAUCE

1 3 lb. chicken, cut up
1 t salt
¼ t freshly ground black pepper
4 T flour
4 T olive oil
2 medium onions, sliced
1 cup chicken broth
¾ cup dry sherry
1 bay leaf
2 T chopped parsley

Rub chicken with salt and pepper, coat with flour. Heat oil in a large skillet, add chicken pieces and brown on all sides, remove. Add onions to skillet and cook until browned, stirring frequently. Return chicken to skillet; add chicken broth, sherry, bay leaf and parsley. Cook until chicken is tender, about 45 minutes. Taste for seasoning; remove chicken to a platter. Pour almond sauce over chicken; garnish with egg white, pimentos and minced parsley.

Almond Sauce:

2 hard-boiled eggs
1 garlic clove, finely minced
2 T flour
12 blanched almonds, finely chopped
½ t salt
¼ t black pepper
Gravy from cooked chicken

Cut whites of eggs in strips and set aside for garnish. Mash yolks, add garlic, flour, almonds, salt and pepper. Blend in some gravy from skillet to form a paste. Stir egg yolk mixture into gravy in skillet; simmer until sauce is thickened.

Garnish:

Reserved egg white strips
¼ cup sliced pimentos
¼ cup minced parsley

A sophisticated African method of preparing chicken is with sweet potatoes and bananas

CHICKEN WITH SWEET POTATOES AND BANANAS

6 T oil
1 2½ lb. chicken, cut into serving pieces
1 medium onion, chopped
1 garlic clove, finely minced
2 T flour
1 cup dry white wine
¾ cup water
1 t salt
½ t black pepper
1 bay leaf
2 small tomatoes, sliced
2 medium, sweet potatoes, peeled and cut in 1½-inch cubes
4 medium, firm bananas, peeled and sliced lengthwise

In a large skillet heat 4 tablespoons oil over medium heat. Add chicken, onion and garlic; cook, turning chicken often until crisp. Sprinkle with flour, add wine, water, salt, pepper, bay leaf and sliced tomatoes. Cover and cook over low heat for 30 minutes. Add sweet potatoes, cover and continue cooking for 30 minutes or until potatoes and chicken are tender. In another skillet, heat 2 tablespoons oil and sauté bananas until golden. Arrange chicken and potatoes on a serving platter and place sautéed bananas around chicken. Pour pan liquid into a bowl and serve as additional sauce.

A North American favorite on a cold rainy day, hearty chicken and corn chowder

CHICKEN AND CORN CHOWDER

2 lbs. chicken parts, breasts, legs and thighs
1 cup water
2 T chopped parsley
2 T chopped celery leaves
2 t salt
2 medium carrots, thinly sliced
2 medium potatoes, pared and cubed
2 stalks celery, sliced
2 cups tomato sauce
1 medium tomato, finely minced
2 cups cream style corn
½ t poultry seasoning

In a large saucepan or Dutch oven combine chicken, water, parsley, celery leaves and 1 teaspoon salt; cover and simmer 30 minutes. Add carrots, potatoes, celery and 1 teaspoon salt; simmer until chicken and vegetables are tender, about 20 minutes. Stir in tomato sauce, tomato, corn and poultry seasoning; simmer, stirring occasionally, for another 15 minutes. Taste for seasoning, serve piping hot.

Although chicken chop suey did not originate in China, but in the United States, it is a favorite everywhere; strips of chicken with crunchy vegetables

CHICKEN CHOP SUEY

3 T oil
4 cups cooked chicken, cut in strips
2 cups sliced fresh mushrooms
1 cup celery, sliced diagonally
½ cup carrots, sliced diagonally
½ cup bean sprouts
2 green onions, thinly sliced
1 t salt
¼ t black pepper
1 cup chicken broth
2 T cornstarch
1 T soy sauce
½ cup water

Heat oil in a large skillet, mix in chicken, mushrooms, celery, carrots, bean sprouts, green onions, salt and pepper. Add chicken broth; cover and simmer over low heat for 5 minutes. Push mixture to one side of skillet. Blend cornstarch, soy sauce and water; slowly stir into liquid in skillet. Cook, stirring constantly until sauce thickens and becomes clear. Taste for seasoning. Excellent served over hot rice or crisp fried noodles.

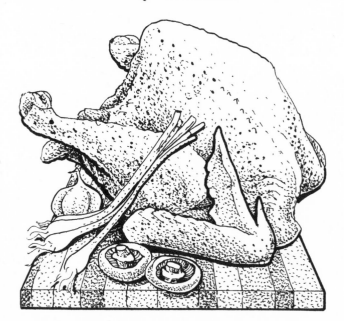

Kota Kapama, the Greek way of preparing chicken in a unique tomato and cinnamon sauce

CHICKEN IN TOMATO AND CINNAMON SAUCE

4 T butter
3 T olive oil
1 3 lb. chicken, cut up
1 t salt
¼ t freshly ground black pepper
1½ cups finely chopped onion
1 T finely minced garlic
1 cup cooked plum tomatoes, chopped
2 T tomato paste
½ cup chicken broth
1 4-inch long cinnamon stick
Freshly grated Parmesan cheese

Warm butter and oil in a large heavy skillet over moderate heat. Season chicken with salt and pepper, brown a few pieces at a time quickly and evenly. As pieces brown, transfer them to a plate. Pour off all but a small amount of oil from skillet, add onions and garlic; stirring frequently, sauté for about 5 minutes. Stir in tomatoes, tomato paste, chicken broth and cinnamon. Bring to a boil, add chicken and baste thoroughly with sauce. Reduce heat to low, cover tightly and simmer, basting occasionally until chicken is tender, about 30 minutes. Taste for seasoning. To serve, arrange chicken on a heated platter and spoon sauce over. Accompany chicken with a small bowl of grated Parmesan cheese. Traditionally the chicken is served with a hot cooked pasta.

An unusual and delicious combination is Armenian Havav Kchuch, a casserole combining chicken breasts, eggplant, tomato, zucchini and green peppers seasoned to perfection

CASSEROLE OF CHICKEN WITH VEGETABLES

1 medium eggplant, cut crosswise in 1-inch slices
4½ t salt
6 T olive oil
2 large whole chicken breasts, cut in half
Freshly ground black pepper
2 medium zucchini, sliced 1-inch thick
2 large green bell peppers, quartered and seeded
2 large tomatoes, sliced
2 garlic cloves, finely minced
3 T finely minced parsley

Sprinkle eggplant slices with 3 teaspoons salt and layer in a collander, cover with a plate and weigh down with a heavy object. Let stand 30 minutes. Rinse and dry thoroughly with paper towels. In a skillet heat 2 tablespoons oil and sauté chicken on both sides until golden brown. Place chicken in a casserole and sprinkle with ½ teaspoon salt and a few grindings of black pepper. In the same skillet, sauté eggplant until golden on both sides, adding more oil as necessary. Place over chicken in casserole. Sauté zucchini in the same manner and place over eggplant; sprinkle with ½ teaspoon salt and a few grindings of black pepper. Sauté green peppers and place over zucchini. Cover with tomato slices and sprinkle top with minced garlic, ½ teaspoon salt and a few grindings of black pepper. Cover and bake in a 350° preheated oven for 1 hour. Garnish with minced parsley. Delicious served with rice pilaf.

Csirke Paprikăs, better known as chicken paprika, an Hungarian favorite made with chicken in a delicious sauce of sour cream, onion and paprika

CHICKEN PAPRIKA

2 T butter
1 3 lb. chicken, cut up
1 medium onion, chopped
1 garlic clove, finely minced
4 t paprika
¾ cup chicken broth
1 t salt
¼ t freshly ground black pepper
1 T flour
1 cup sour cream

In a large skillet heat butter and fry chicken on both sides until golden. Remove as cooked and keep warm. When all pieces are cooked, add onion and garlic to pan drippings and sauté until tender. Stir in paprika and cook 1 minute. Add chicken broth, salt and pepper; bring to a boil. Return chicken to skillet; cover and cook slowly until chicken is tender, about 40 minutes. Remove chicken to a warm platter. Combine flour and sour cream, mix into the skillet. Cook slowly, stirring constantly, until thickened and smooth. Taste for seasoning. Return chicken pieces to sauce and heat thoroughly, do not allow to boil.

Bulgarian Jachnia, is a whole chicken stewed with fresh tomatoes, onions and wine

CHICKEN STEWED WITH VEGETABLES AND WINE

4 T butter
1 whole 3 lb. chicken
4 medium onions, sliced
1 garlic clove, finely minced

4 large tomatoes, peeled and quartered
3 t paprika
1 t salt
¼ t freshly ground black pepper
Dry white wine, about 2 cups

Heat butter in a heavy casserole dish and fry chicken until browned on all sides. Remove chicken to a plate. To casserole, add onion, garlic, tomatoes, paprika, salt and pepper; sauté for 5 minutes. Return chicken to sauce in casserole and add wine to cover ingredients. Bring to a boil, cover, lower heat and slowly simmer until chicken is tender, about 1 hour. Taste for seasoning. Remove chicken to a platter, cut into serving pieces and cover with vegetable sauce.

A French recipe, Poulet à la Vallee D'Auge is chicken cooked with pieces of apple in a delicate cream sauce

CHICKEN WITH APPLES

5 T butter
1 3 lb. chicken, cut up
1 t salt
¼ t black pepper
4 T minced onion
2 large apples, peeled and cut in eighths
1 cup apple cider
¼ t thyme
½ cup heavy cream

Melt butter in a casserole dish. Season chicken with salt and pepper and brown in butter. Add onions and apples, cook 5 minutes. Add cider and thyme; cover and cook over low heat until chicken is tender, about 45 minutes. Arrange chicken on a heated platter. Stir cream into the sauce; heat, but do not allow to boil. Taste for seasoning. Pour over chicken

A very continental recipe from Mexico City, chicken with avocados, wine and almonds

CHICKEN WITH AVOCADO

2½ lbs. chicken breasts or thighs
2 T flour
1 t salt
¼ t black pepper
3 T oil
1 medium onion, finely chopped
1 garlic clove, finely minced
½ cup chopped green bell pepper
2 stalks celery, chopped
⅛ t cumin
⅛ t paprika
½ cup chicken broth
½ cup dry sherry
½ cup chopped pimento
¼ cup sliced blanched almonds
2 medium firm avocados, peeled and diced

Coat chicken pieces in mixture of flour, salt and black pepper. In heavy skillet lightly brown chicken in oil. Add onion, garlic, green pepper and celery; cover and let simmer 5 minutes. Add cumin, paprika, chicken broth and sherry; cover and simmer until chicken is tender, about 45 minutes. Add pimento, almonds and avocado, distributing carefully to avoid breaking the chicken pieces. Taste for seasoning; simmer a few minutes more.

A tempting Greek preparation of chicken breasts cooked with wine and yogurt

GREEK CHICKEN AND YOGURT

4 small whole chicken breasts
4 T lemon juice
1 small garlic clove, crushed
¾ t salt
¼ t black pepper
½ t poultry seasoning
5 T butter
1 large onion, sliced
⅛ t nutmeg
1 cup rosé wine
2 cups chicken broth
2 cups plain yogurt
3 T flour

Rub chicken breasts with lemon juice, garlic, salt, pepper and poultry seasoning. Melt butter in a large skillet, add chicken and brown. Place onion slices underneath browned chicken and cook 5 minutes. Sprinkle chicken with nutmeg. Add wine and 1 cup chicken broth; bring to a boil, reduce heat. Combine yogurt and flour; add remaining chicken broth which has been heated, stir thoroughly to eliminate lumps. Gradually add yogurt mixture to chicken, mixing well. Place skillet lid slightly ajar and cook until chicken is tender, about 1 hour. Taste for seasoning. Delicious served over rice.

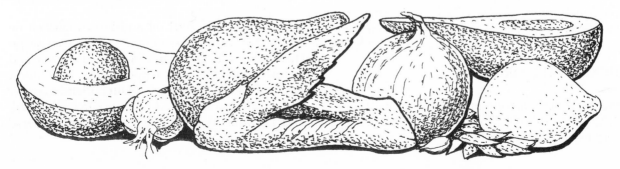

Chinese stir-fry method of preparing chicken with mushrooms, pod peas, celery cabbage, served over rice and garnished with almonds

CHICKEN WITH MUSHROOMS

1 T oil
2 large whole chicken breasts, skinned and boned, cut in
    1-inch cubes
1 t salt
½ t black pepper
2 cups Chinese pod peas
1 cup shredded celery cabbage
4 cups sliced mushrooms
½ cup chicken broth
2 T cornstarch
2 t soy sauce
¼ cup water
2 cups hot cooked rice
½ cup almonds

In a wok or large frying pan heat oil; add chicken, salt and pepper. Cook chicken until almost tender; add pea pods, celery cabbage and mushrooms. Add chicken broth and cook covered over moderate flame for 10 minutes. Blend together cornstarch, soy sauce and water; add mixture and cook 5 minutes more, stirring constantly. Serve immediately over hot rice and sprinkle with almonds.

A traditional Japanese delight is Chicken Yakitori; pieces of chicken, green onions and green peppers barbecued on skewers over a grill with a sesame seed sauce

CHICKEN YAKITORI

4 medium whole chicken breasts, boned, skinned and
    each breast cut in 8 pieces
8 green onions, cut in 2-inch pieces
2 medium green bell peppers, cut in 1½-inch squares
½ cup sesame seed oil
½ cup sesame seeds
2 T lemon juice
2 T soy sauce

Arrange chicken pieces, green onions and green peppers alternately on 8 skewers. Place sesame seed oil, sesame seeds, lemon juice and soy sauce in a blender; puree until smooth. Brush chicken skewers with sesame sauce. Broil chicken on a grill over hot coals or in oven broiler about 8-10 minutes on each side, basting several times with sesame sauce during cooking.

An easy to prepare, tasty Malayan chicken cooked with olives, water chestnuts, wine, orange juice and ginger

MALAYAN CHICKEN

4 T oil
1 3 lb. chicken, cut up
1 cup dry white wine
½ cup orange juice
½ cup halved pitted ripe black olives
½ cup sliced water chestnuts
1 t salt
1 small garlic clove crushed
1 t ginger
2 T cornstarch
2 T water

In a large skillet, heat oil and brown chicken on both sides. Add wine, orange juice, olives, water chestnuts, salt, garlic and ginger; stir, cover and simmer until chicken is tender, about 45 minutes. Remove chicken to a warm platter. Blend together cornstarch and water, add to sauce in skillet; cook and stir until thickened, taste for seasoning. Serve with chicken.

Puerto Ricans enjoy dining on Arroz con Pollo, chicken cooked in a savory sauce with rice, beautifully garnished with green peas and strips of red pimento

CHICKEN WITH RICE

½ t oregano, crumbled
2 garlic cloves, finely minced
1½ t salt
2 large tomatoes, chopped
1 medium green bell pepper, chopped
1 medium onion, chopped
1 3 lb. chicken, cut up
¼ t saffron
1 cup uncooked rice
¼ cup pitted green olives
1 T capers
1¼ cup chicken broth
1 cup cooked fresh green peas
¼ cup pimento strips

Mix oregano, garlic and salt; rub well into chicken pieces. In a heavy skillet cook tomatoes, peppers and onion for 5 minutes. Add chicken; cover and simmer slowly for 30 minutes. Mix in saffron, rice, olives, capers and chicken broth. Bring to a boil, stirring constantly; lower heat, cover and cook until rice is done and all liquid is absorbed, about 30 minutes. Serve on a warmed platter; garnish with green peas and strips of pimento.

A pungently savory, yet simple to prepare Indian eggplant and chicken curry

EGGPLANT AND CHICKEN CURRY

1 T curry powder
1 t paprika
1½ t salt
2½ lbs. chicken parts, skin removed
3 T oil
1 eggplant, about 1-lb., quartered and thinly sliced
1 large onion, cut in half and thinly sliced
1 medium green bell pepper, sliced in thin strips
1 garlic clove, finely minced
¾ cup tomato juice

Mix curry powder, paprika and 1 teaspoon of salt. Roll chicken pieces in mixture. In a large skillet heat oil; add chicken and brown, remove chicken. Add eggplant, onion, green pepper, garlic, tomato juice and ½ teaspoon of salt to skillet. Mix well and place chicken over vegetable mixture. Cover and simmer until chicken is tender, about 45 minutes. Excellent served with rice.

Armenians prepare Bdoughov Hav, a delicately different combination of chicken, apricots, prunes and raisins gently flavored with cinnamon

CHICKEN WITH APRICOTS, PRUNES AND RAISINS

4 T butter
4 small whole chicken breasts
1 t cinnamon
½ t salt
1⅔ cups hot water
1 cup dried apricots
1 cup dried prunes
1 cup seedless golden raisins
2 T sugar

In a heavy skillet melt butter and sauté chicken on both sides until lightly brown. Sprinkle with cinnamon and salt; add hot water, cover and simmer 15 minutes. Add apricots, prunes, raisins and sugar. Continue cooking over low heat until the chicken is tender, about 40 minutes. Excellent served with rice pilaf.

Iranian's prepare a most delicious combination of chicken and mushrooms in a wine and sour cream sauce served over bulgur pilaf

CHICKEN IRAN OVER BULGUR PILAF

4 T butter
1 medium onion, sliced
1 garlic clove, finely minced
3 whole chicken breasts, boned, skinned and cut in 3-inch strips
1 t salt
½ t thyme
¼ t black pepper
½ cup dry white wine
2 cups fresh mushrooms, cut in halves
¼ cup sliced red pimento
1 T flour
½ cup sour cream

In a large skillet heat 2 tablespoons butter and sauté onion and garlic until tender, about 3 minutes. With slotted spoon remove onion and set aside. Add chicken strips to skillet and sauté lightly. Add salt, thyme and black pepper; continue cooking until chicken is lightly browned. Add wine, cover and simmer 15 minutes. In a saucepan melt 2 tablespoons butter and sauté mushrooms until just tender. Add mushrooms, onion and pimento to chicken. Stir flour into sour cream; add to chicken. Stir and cook until slightly thickened; do not allow to boil. Taste for seasoning. Serve over bulgur pilaf.

Bulgur Pilaf:

2 cups chicken broth
3 T butter
1 cup bulgur (coarse cracked wheat)
Salt to taste

In a saucepan bring chicken broth to a boil; add butter and bulgur. Taste, if necessary add salt. Cover and simmer over medium-low heat, about 15 minutes or until all moisture is absorbed. Fluff gently with a fork and serve.

Chinese style green peppers stuffed with chicken, rice and water chestnuts

CHICKEN-STUFFED GREEN PEPPERS

4 large green bell peppers
2 cups chicken broth
2 T cornstarch
1 T chopped parsley
1 t soy sauce
½ t marjoram
¼ t salt
2 small whole chicken breasts, cooked, boned and diced in 1-inch cubes
1 cup cooked rice
½ cup sliced celery
½ cup sliced water chestnuts
¼ cup sliced green onions

Using a small sharp knife, cut a wide circle around stem of each pepper and lift off. Scoop out core and seeds. Blanch peppers in boiling water for 2 minutes; drain well. Combine chicken broth, cornstarch, half of parsley, soy sauce, marjoram and salt in a small saucepan. Cook and stir until sauce comes to a boil and thickens. Combine chicken, rice, celery, water chestnuts and green onions with ¾ cup of the sauce. Taste for seasoning. Fill peppers with chicken-rice mixture and place in a shallow casserole. Bake in a 350° preheated oven for 30 minutes. Keep remaining sauce warm and pour over peppers before serving. Sprinkle with remaining parsley.

*An elegant French recipe for Roquefort cheese lovers,
Poulet a la mode de Roquefort, chicken halves baked with
a cover of cheese and sour cream*

CHICKEN WITH ROQUEFORT CHEESE

2 1½ lb. broiling chickens, split
1½ t salt
¼ t freshly ground black pepper
3 T butter
1 cup crumbled Roquefort cheese
1 garlic clove, finely minced
1½ cup sour cream

Rub chicken halves with salt and pepper. Melt butter in a skillet and brown the chickens. Remove and arrange in a baking dish, single layer. Mash cheese with a fork and blend with garlic and sour cream. Spread over the chicken. Cover and bake in a 375° preheated oven until chicken is tender, about 30 minutes. Uncover and bake 5 minutes.

*Coq au Vin is a classic French dish, chicken cooked in
wine with mushrooms and small whole white onions*

CHICKEN WITH WINE

1 3 lb. chicken, cut up
1 t salt
2 T flour
1 small onion, chopped
3 T butter
3 cups dry red wine
3 cups chicken broth
1 bay leaf
2 sprigs parsley
1 sprig fresh or 1 t dried marjoram
1 garlic clove, slightly crushed

12 small white boiling onions, peeled
2 cups small whole mushrooms

Rub the chicken with salt and flour. In a heavy pan, cook chopped onion in butter. Add chicken and brown well. Pour in wine and chicken broth. Add herb bouquet made by tying together in a piece of cheesecloth the bayleaf, parsley, marjoram and garlic. Place boiling onions and mushrooms around chicken. Cover pan and simmer slowly until chicken is tender, about 1 hour. Remove herb bouquet from sauce. Taste for seasoning. Traditionally served with warm crusty French bread.

*In Nigeria, chicken is cooked with a most unique sauce of
peanut and hard-boiled eggs, served over rice*

NIGERIAN CHICKEN

1 2½ lb. chicken, cut up
1 medium onion, chopped
1 large tomato, finely chopped
2 garlic cloves, finely minced
1 t salt
1 T tomato paste
3 cups water
¾ cup crunchy peanut butter
⅛ t cayenne pepper
3 hard-boiled eggs, sliced
2 cups hot cooked rice

In a large skillet combine chicken, onion, tomato, garlic, salt, tomato paste and 2 cups of water. Bring to a boil, cover and simmer for 30 minutes. Mix together peanut butter, cayenne pepper and 1 cup water. Add to chicken, cover and simmer slowly for 45 minutes, stirring occasionally. Taste for seasoning. Add sliced hard-boiled eggs. Serve over rice.

Chicken and dumplings is a favorite in the Southern United States, chicken, vegetables and plump delicate dumplings in a rich flavorful gravy

CHICKEN STEW WITH DUMPLINGS

1 3 lb. chicken, cut up
6 cups boiling water
1 T salt
½ t poultry seasoning
1 medium carrot, thinly sliced
1 cup chopped celery
4 small potatoes, peeled
8 small white boiling onions, peeled
2 T cornstarch
4 T cold water
Parsley sprigs

Place chicken in a large covered pan; add boiling water, salt and poultry seasoning. Bring to a boil; cover, lower heat and simmer slowly for 1 hour. Remove chicken and strain broth. Add water to broth to make 6 cups. Return broth to pan, add carrot, celery, potatoes and onions; cook another 10 minutes. Drop, ½ teaspoon of the dumpling batter at a time into the broth. Cover; boil for 10 minutes exactly. Mix together cornstarch and cold water and gently stir into simmering pot. Add chicken; continue to simmer and stir gently until chicken is hot and gravy rich and clear. Serve immediately; spoon onto serving platter and garnish with sprigs of parsley.

Dumplings:

¾ cup flour
½ t baking powder
½ t salt
1 egg, beaten
¼ cup milk

Sift together flour, baking powder and salt. Combine together egg and milk; blend into flour mixture, making a soft sticky dough.

The Polynesians prepare chicken breasts in a delicate aromatic sauce of pineapple and orange juice, garnished with papaya slices

PAPAYA CHICKEN

4 T butter
4 small whole chicken breasts, split in half
½ t salt
⅛ t black pepper
¼ t paprika
1 cup pineapple-orange juice concentrate
1 t soy sauce
½ t ginger
2 garlic cloves, crushed
¼ cup water
1 large papaya, peeled and sliced in wedges

Heat butter in a frying pan. Season chicken breasts with salt, pepper and paprika, sauté in butter until browned on both sides. Arrange chicken in a baking pan. In a saucepan heat together pineapple-orange juice concentrate, soy sauce, ginger, garlic and water. Spoon all but ¼ cup of sauce over chicken. Bake in a 350° preheated oven until tender, about 30 minutes; baste frequently with sauce from around chicken. If necessary, add a few spoonfuls of water to sauce to keep chicken moist. Dip papaya slices in reserved ¼ cup sauce and place on top of chicken. Continue baking for another 5 minutes.

Poulet a l'ail is a simple, yet gourmet French provincial delight of chicken baked with cloves of garlic which you "suck out" and enjoy with the roasted chicken.

ROASTED CHICKEN AND CLOVES OF GARLIC

1 3 lb. chicken, quartered
1 t salt
½ t black pepper
2 T butter, melted
20 unpeeled garlic cloves (yes, twenty cloves)
½ cup water

Place chicken quarters in a roasting pan in one layer. Season with salt and pepper; drizzle melted butter over chicken. Place unpeeled garlic cloves around chicken. Bake chicken in a 400° preheated oven for 60 minutes or until golden and fork-tender; basting every 10 minutes. Remove chicken to a warmed serving platter. Add water to roasting pan with garlic cloves and boil 1 to 2 minutes over direct heat to melt all the solidified juices. Pour sauce and garlic cloves over chicken. Serve chicken pieces with the garlic cloves and some of the natural sauce.

New Orleans chicken jambalaya baked with rice, tomatoes, onions, green pepper and celery

CHICKEN JAMBALAYA

1 large onion, chopped
4 T oil
1 medium green bell pepper, chopped
½ cup chopped celery
2 cups cooked tomatoes
1 cup tomato sauce
1 t salt
¼ t freshly ground black pepper
1½ cup cooked rice
2 cups diced cooked chicken
3 T fine dry bread crumbs blended with 1 T melted butter
¼ cup minced parsley
¼ cup green onion slices

In a skillet sauté onion in oil for a few minutes. Add green pepper, celery, tomato, tomato sauce, salt and black pepper; cook 5 minutes. Add rice and chicken; stir to mix all ingredients. Taste for seasoning. Turn into a baking dish; top with buttered crumbs. Bake in a 350° preheated oven for 30 minutes. Garnish with minced parsley and green onion slices.

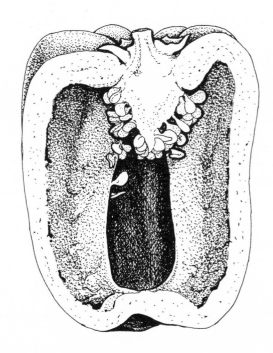

A delicious Oriental stir-fry chicken with walnuts, celery, bamboo shoots and water chestnuts

ORIENTAL WALNUT CHICKEN

4 T oil
1 cup coarsely broken walnuts
2 whole uncooked chicken breasts, boned and cut in thin
    strips
½ t salt
1 medium onion, sliced
1½ cups celery, diagonally sliced
1¼ cups chicken broth
1 t sugar
1 T cornstarch
4 T soy sauce
2 T dry sherry
½ cup bamboo shoots
½ cup sliced water chestnuts

Heat oil in a wok or large skillet, add walnuts and cook for a few minutes, remove walnuts. Add chicken to skillet and sprinkle with salt; cook, stirring frequently until tender, about 10 minutes. Remove chicken. Add onion, celery and ½ cup of chicken broth; cook uncovered 5 minutes. Combine sugar, cornstarch, soy sauce, sherry and ¾ cup chicken broth, pour over vegetables; cook and stir until sauce thickens. Add chicken, bamboo shoots, water chestnuts and walnuts; heat through. Excellent served over hot cooked rice.

Japanese chicken teriyaki, chicken pieces marinated in a flavorful sauce enhanced with papaya and broiled, preferably over charcoal

CHICKEN TERIYAKI

½ ripe papaya, mashed
¾ cup chopped onion
2 garlic cloves, finely minced
1 small piece ginger root, mashed

2½ T brown sugar
1½ cups soy sauce
1 cup water
2 T Sake or dry sherry
3 lbs. chicken pieces

Mix all ingredients except chicken. Marinate chicken in sauce for at least 3 hours. Broil chicken, basting occasionally with marinade until tender, about 45 minutes.

A California recipe for chicken cooked with orange juice and with the interesting addition of raisins and macadamia nuts

ORANGE CHICKEN

2½ lbs. chicken pieces
1 t salt
4 T butter
2 T flour
1 T brown sugar
½ t curry powder
⅛ t cinnamon
1 small piece ginger root, minced or ½ t powdered ginger
1½ cups orange juice
½ cup raisins
½ cup chopped macadamia nuts
1 medium orange, peeled and sectioned

Sprinkle chicken with ½ teaspoon salt. In a large skillet, heat butter and brown chicken; remove from pan. Mix flour, sugar, curry powder, cinnamon, and ½ teaspoon salt; stir into pan drippings to form a smooth paste. Add ginger and bubbles and begins to thicken. Return chicken to skillet, add raisins; cover and cook over low heat until chicken is tender, about 45 minutes. Sprinkle with nuts and orange sections; cook another 5 minutes. Taste for seasoning. Excellent served over hot cooked rice.

Who has not heard of the loving and healing quality of a steaming bowl of Jewish chicken soup with matzo dumplings

CHICKEN SOUP WITH MATZO DUMPLINGS

1 2½ lb. chicken, cut up
8 cups water
2 medium onions, chopped
4 medium carrots, peeled and sliced
2 stalks celery with tops, sliced
1 medium parsnip, peeled and sliced
4 sprigs parsley
1 T salt
¼ t black pepper

Place chicken in a large kettle; add water, onions, carrots, celery, parsnips, parsley, salt and pepper. Cover and simmer for 1½-hours. Add a little more water if necessary and simmer, uncovered for another 20 minutes. With slotted spoon remove chicken from soup. Pull meat from bones and return to soup, discarding bones. Taste for seasoning, add salt if necessary. Bring soup to a rapid boil and drop in matzo dumplings by the spoonful. Cover and simmer for 20 minutes; do not uncover while dumplings are cooking. Serve at once.

Matzo Dumplings:

3 eggs, separated
¾ cup water
1 t salt
⅛ t black pepper
1 cup matzo meal

Place egg yolks, water, salt and pepper in a bowl and beat with a fork. Beat egg whites until stiff, but not dry. Gently fold matzo meal and egg yolk mixture into the whites until blended. Let rest, covered, 15 minutes. Makes 12 dumplings.

A unique combination is this Vietnamese chicken salad, Goi Ga, made with thin strips of chicken and shredded cabbage with a tangy ginger flavor

CHICKEN AND CABBAGE SALAD

4 green onions
2 large chicken breasts, skinned and boned, cut in matchstick-size strips
1 t finely minced fresh ginger
2 t salt
1 t black pepper
8 T salad oil
6 T lemon juice
1 t sugar
6 cups finely shredded cabbage

Cut green tops of onions in thin strips, then in 2-inch lengths; set aside. Finely chop white part of onions; combine with chicken, ginger, 1 teaspoon salt and ½ teaspoon pepper. Pour 4 tablespoons oil in a large skillet and place over high heat. When oil is hot, add chicken mixture. Stirring constantly, cook until chicken is no longer pink, about 5 to 6 minutes. Let mixture cool completely. Combine lemon juice, sugar, 1 teaspoon salt, ½ teaspoon pepper and 4 tablespoons oil. Just before serving, toss together chicken, lemon juice mixture and shredded cabbage; garnish with green onion strips.

Cantonese chicken baked in a seasoning of honey, soy sauce and catsup, enhanced with tangy slices of pineapple

CANTONESE CHICKEN

1 3 lb. chicken, cut up
½ cup tomato catsup
3 T honey
3 T soy sauce
2 T lemon juice
1 T cornstarch
2 T water
4 pineapple slices

In a large baking pan arrange chicken pieces in a single layer, skin side up. Mix together catsup, honey, soy sauce, and lemon juice; pour over chicken pieces and marinate for at least 2 hours. Cover pan with foil and bake in a 375° preheated oven for 30 minutes. Uncover pan and baste with sauce; continue baking until chicken is tender, about 30 minutes. Pour pan juices in a saucepan and bring to a boil. Mix together cornstarch and water and stir in, cooking until sauce is thickened. Arrange chicken on a serving platter. Garnish with pineapple slices. Spoon sauce over chicken and serve immediately.

California is noted for oranges and almonds, which combine deliciously with chicken for an elegant main dish

ALMOND CHICKEN IN ORANGE SAUCE

1 t paprika
1 t salt
¼ t black pepper
1 3 lb. chicken, cut up
5 T butter
1 cup orange juice
⅔ cup slivered almonds, toasted
1 medium orange, thinly sliced
¼ cup finely minced parsley

Rub paprika, salt and pepper into chicken. In a large frying pan, heat butter and sauté chicken on both sides until golden brown. Cover, reduce heat and cook until chicken is tender, about 30 minutes. Remove chicken to platter and keep warm. Add orange juice to frying pan. Stir to loosen all the browned particles; cook over high heat until liquid is reduced by half. Pour sauce over chicken and sprinkle with toasted almonds. Garnish with orange slices and top with finely minced parsley.

Easy to prepare, pungently seasoned, marinated chicken curry becomes Vindaloo from India

CHICKEN CURRY

2 t tumeric
2 t coriander
2 t cumin
1 t dry mustard
¼ t cayenne pepper
1 t salt
½ cup vinegar
1 3 lb. chicken, cut up
2 large onions, chopped
2 T oil

Combine tumeric, coriander, cumin, mustard, cayenne, salt and vinegar. Place chicken in a shallow dish with spice-vinegar mixture. Cover; refrigerate 6 to 7 hours, spooning marinade over chicken occasionally. In a skillet, cook onion in oil until tender but not brown. Add chicken and marinade. Cover and simmer until chicken is tender, about 45 minutes.

An easy to prepare, Spanish style hearty chicken dish with garbanzo beans and wine, baked in foil. Ideal to serve for an outdoor patio meal

CHICKEN WITH GARBANZO BEANS

1 large onion, chopped
1 stalk celery with leaves, chopped
1 3 lb. chicken, quartered
3 T olive oil
2 cups cooked garbanzo beans
1 t salt
½ t freshly ground black pepper
½ t oregano
1½ cups tomato sauce
½ cup Burgundy wine

Place a large sheet of heavy duty foil on a shallow pan. Add onion and celery and then chicken, skin side down. Brush chicken with olive oil. Brown lightly under broiler; turn chicken once and brush with oil. Remove from broiler and bring up edges of foil. Add garbanzo beans and sprinkle with salt, pepper and oregano. Blend together tomato sauce and wine; pour over chicken. Close foil to make a tight package. Return to oven and bake in a 350° preheated oven, about 1½ hours. Serve from the foil with warm crusty bread and a crisp green salad.

vegetables and grains

Vegetables add variety and nutrition to meals. They give color, flavor and texture, as well as providing generous amounts of important vitamins and minerals. Most vegetables are low in calories. The appreciation of vegetables as food has greatly increased in recent years with a firmer understanding of their value to a well-balanced diet. Usually fresh vegetables have their best taste and flavor and cost less when they are the most plentiful, so prepare recipes with vegetables at the height of their season. Today we know that legumes are a good source of protein, and when combined with milk or cheese as part of the menu, serve as a substitute for meat, fish or poultry. Grains are basic in the daily diet of many peoples around the world. Bulgur, a cracked whole-wheat, is favored in the Middle East countries; Russians and Israelis enjoy buckwheat groats cooked into a porridge called *kasha*. Romanians delight in a corn meal mush called *mamaliga,* served in a variety of ways. In Italy, wheat is prepared in various forms of pasta. The Far East and India enjoy rice; the Polish, a nutty-flavored barley. These wholesome and flavorful grains add a robust flavor to a meal. Be adventuresome by preparing national foods or regional dishes from around the world. It will make your cooking more imaginative and eating more pleasurable.

Selection of Vegetables

When purchasing vegetables, select the freshest, youngest vegetables you can buy. Head vegetables should be solid to the touch; leafy vegetables should be crisp. Peas and beans should have crisp pods. Buy only the amount of vegetables you will be using within a few days; they deteriorate in quality and flavor.

Washing and Preparation of Vegetables

Clean spinach and other leafy greens thoroughly. Cut off and discard tough stems, roots and bruised leaves. Rinse and clean in water by lifting up and down several times, changing the water frequently. In tightly-grown vegetables such as cauliflower, broccoli, artichokes and cabbage, soak in cold water for 20 to 30 minutes before using. Mushrooms should never be soaked or washed, simply wiped clean with a damp paper towel.

Leave edible peel on vegetables such as young carrots and zucchini; wash and scrub well with a brush. When vegetables must be peeled, keep parings as thin as possible; many minerals and vitamins are located just under the skin. To peel tomatoes, dip in boiling water 1 minute, then in cold water; skin will remove easily. Beets will also quickly peel if you dip them in cold water immediately after they are boiled.

In preparing cooked vegetables for recipes, they may be cooked waterless, steamed or boiled; but most importantly kept crisp and tender; never soft, shapeless or mushy. Spinach is best cooked waterless and slowly, in an uncovered saucepan; this helps retain its bright green color. Vegetables may be steamed, using a special steaming utensil placed in a deep kettle with a small amount of water. This is an excellent method since the water does not come in contact with the vegetables. Boiled vegetables should never be cooked in vast amounts of water, since minerals and vitamins are dissolved in the water. It is better to use a heavy-bottom saucepan with a tight-fitting cover making it possible to cook vegetables in much less water. By adding 1 teaspoon vinegar to water when boiling potatoes they will remain extra white without the usual discoloration. A piece of lemon added to cooking cauliflower will help retain its whiteness.

Storage of Vegetables

Before refrigerating vegetables such as lettuce, spinach, celery, carrots, parsley and radishes, they should be washed in cold water, drained thoroughly and patted dry with paper towels until all moisture is removed. Refrigerate in sealed plastic bags or covered containers until ready to use.

Store refrigerated and covered until ready to use asparagus, beans, beets, broccoli, cabbage, carrots, cauliflower, celery, cucumbers, salad greens, peas, green peppers, radishes, turnips and zucchini.

Store refrigerated and uncovered ripe avocados, unhusked corn, peas and beans in pods, tomatoes and eggplant.

Store in a cool, dry, well-ventilated place without washing potatoes, onions, garlic, rutabagas, winter squash, sweet potatoes and yams.

Vegetables and Grains

Mamaliga, a cornmeal porridge, is a favorite staple of Romanians, served with the meal in a variety of ways

CORNMEAL PORRIDGE

½ t salt
2½ cups water
1 cup yellow cornmeal

In a covered saucepan, heat salted water to boiling. Slowly add cornmeal, stirring vigorously with a wooden spoon until mixture is thick and smooth. Cover and simmer over low heat for 12 minutes or until meal takes the shape of pan. Run a wet knife around edges and invert on a plate. Traditionally served hot with fish, chicken or vegetable stews, sauce or gravy is spooned over mamaliga.

Other serving suggestions:

1. Serve hot with melted butter, sour cream, grated cheese or topped with fried eggs.
2. Leftover cool mamaliga is sometimes cut into slices, dipped in beaten egg, sprinkled with grated cheese and fried in butter until golden brown. Serve with yogurt or sour cream.

Tian is a French peasant casserole made with spinach and zucchini, baked with eggs and cheese. Serve as a side dish or double recipe to serve as an entree

VEGETABLE TIAN

2 T olive oil
1 bunch spinach, chopped
3 medium zucchini, diced
1 small onion, chopped
1 garlic clove, finely minced
½ t basil
½ t salt
½ t black pepper
4 eggs, beaten
½ cup grated Swiss cheese
¼ cup bread crumbs

Heat oil in Dutch oven, add spinach; sauté until just wilted. Add zucchini, onion and garlic; cook until barely tender. Add basil, salt and pepper. Pour eggs over vegetables and top with cheese and bread crumbs. Bake in a 350° preheated oven until eggs are set and cheese is melted and bubbly, about 20 minutes.

Plov, a Russian favorite, is rice prepared with dried apricots, raisins and saffron, cooked in a chicken broth.

APRICOT RICE

½ cup dried apricots
¼ cup seedless raisins
1½ cups chicken broth
⅛ t saffron
2 T butter
¾ cup uncooked rice
¾ t salt
⅛ t black pepper

Cover apricots and raisins with boiling water; soak for 2 hours. Drain and cut into bite-sized pieces. In a saucepan bring chicken broth, saffron and butter to a boil. Stir in rice; season with salt and pepper. Add apricots and raisins; mix well. Lower heat, cover and cook slowly until rice is tender, separate, and liquid is absorbed, about 25 minutes.

A Southern United States style of sweet potatoes with apricot halves and spiced with whole cloves

SWEET POTATOES WITH APRICOTS

½ cup drained apricot liquid or apricot nectar
Whole cloves
4 medium sweet potatoes, cooked, peeled and quartered
1½ cups drained apricot halves
1 T butter

Combine apricot liquid and 2 whole cloves. Boil until reduced to ⅓ cup, about 8 to 10 minutes. Place half the sweet potatoes in a casserole; top with half the apricots, repeat layers. Stick a clove into each apricot half on top layer. Pour reduced syrup over and dot with butter. Bake in a 350° preheated oven for 30 minutes.

The Polish usually serve barley, a nutritious nutty-flavored grain, with fish or poultry

BARLEY AND MUSHROOM

1 medium onion, chopped
4 T butter
2 cups sliced fresh mushrooms
1 cup pearl barley
2½ cups chicken broth
1 t salt
¼ t black pepper

In a heavy saucepan, sauté onion in butter until tender. Add mushrooms and sauté about 5 minutes. Stir in barley, add chicken broth, salt and pepper. Bring to a boil, lower heat and cover tightly. Cook until barley is tender and liquid is absorbed, about 1 hour.

Gratin Dauphinois is a French recipe for those who enjoy crunchy potatoes, baked slowly in the oven with cream

CRUNCHY POTATOES

4 large potatoes, peeled and thinly sliced
Salt to taste
Freshly ground black pepper
⅛ t nutmeg
1½ cups light cream
3 T butter

Arrange potatoes in a buttered shallow baking dish, sprinkling salt, pepper and nutmeg between layers. Add cream and dot with small pieces of butter. Bake in a 250° preheated oven until cream is almost absorbed and potatoes are brown, about 1½ hours.

Broccoli Alla Siciliana; broccoli Italian style seasoned with anchovies, olive oil and lemon juice

BROCCOLI WITH ANCHOVIES

4 stalks broccoli, cut in medium-sized pieces
4 T olive oil
1 garlic clove, finely minced
3 fillets of anchovy, cut into small pieces
4 T warm water
½ t salt
4 T lemon juice
Dash of freshly ground black pepper

Cook broccoli; drain. Combine olive oil, garlic and anchovies in a saucepan; heat thoroughly. Add broccoli, warm water and salt; simmer until tender, about 10 minutes. Add lemon juice and dash of pepper. Serve very hot.

Bulgur, a form of cracked wheat, is a staple in Middle Eastern cooking, especially Bulgur Pilaf

BULGUR PILAF

1 small onion, finely minced
3 T olive oil
2½ cups chicken broth
1 t salt
1 cup coarse bulgur

In a saucepan, sauté onion in olive oil until light brown. Remove from heat; add chicken broth and bring to a boil. Add salt and bulgur; bring to a second boil; cover, reduce heat and cook for 30 minutes.

Subzi Kari is an Indian mixed vegetable curry made with potato, carrot, cauliflower, peas and green beans; seasoned with pungent spices

VEGETABLE CURRY

½ cup chopped onion
1 T butter
½ t turmeric
½ t coriander
⅛ t cinnamon
⅛ t ground cloves
⅛ t black pepper
⅛ t cayenne pepper
1 garlic clove, finely minced
½ t grated fresh gingerroot
¾ cup water
2 medium carrots, cut in ½-inch slices
¾ t salt
1 medium potato, peeled and diced
1 cup green peas
1 cup coarsely chopped cauliflower
1 cup green beans, cut in 1-inch pieces
½ cup chopped tomato
1 t lemon juice

In a saucepan, cook and stir onion in butter for a few minutes. Stir in turmeric, coriander, cinnamon, cloves, black pepper and cayenne. Add garlic, gingerroot and water; cook and stir 5 minutes. Add carrots and salt; bring to a boil and simmer covered for 20 minutes. Add potatoes, peas, cauliflower, green beans and tomatoes; bring to a boil; simmer covered, until vegetables are tender-crisp, about 10 minutes. Stir in lemon juice and taste for seasoning.

Mexican Concombres Persilles combines hot cucumber in cream sauce; excellent served with simple poached fish

CUCUMBERS IN PARSLIED CREAM

4 medium cucumbers, peeled and cut into large cubes
3 T butter
½ t salt
¼ t freshly ground black pepper
½ cup cream
1 T finely minced parsley

Remove seeds from cucumber pieces. Cook cucumbers until just tender; drain well. Melt butter in a saucepan until it foams; add cucumbers, salt and pepper; gently sauté for 5 minutes. Add cream and parsley; continue cooking until entire mixture is hot.

The Finnish prepare Punajuripihvit, beet slices dipped in egg and bread crumbs, sautéed in butter

FINNISH BEETS

2 cups cooked sliced beets
1 egg, lightly beaten
½ cup fine dry bread crumbs
2 T butter
1 T lemon juice
2 T chopped parsley

Dip beet slices first in egg, then in bread crumbs. In a skillet sauté beet slices in butter, browning both sides. Remove to a heated platter; sprinkle with lemon juice and chopped parsley.

Mexican Calabazas Rellenas; zucchini stuffed with cream cheese, covered with sour cream and baked

STUFFED ZUCCHINI WITH CREAM CHEESE

4 medium zucchini
3 ounces cream cheese
2 T finely minced onion
¼ t salt
¼ t black pepper
1 cup sour cream
Paprika

Remove stem and blossom ends from zucchini; cook whole until almost tender; drain and cool. Cut each zucchini in half lengthwise; scoop seeds into a small bowl. Mix seeds with cream cheese, onion, salt and pepper. Stuff mixture into the halves. Arrange in a buttered baking dish; spoon sour cream evenly over top and sprinkle with paprika. Bake in a 325° preheated oven until well heated, about 10 minutes.

Zanahorias al Miel is a Chilean recipe for young carrots, honey, mint and Swiss cheese

HONEYED CARROTS WITH SWISS CHEESE

12 young fresh carrots
3 T honey
1 T chopped fresh mint
½ cup grated Swiss cheese

Cook carrots until crisply tender. Split carrots from end to end. Arrange in shallow baking dish and drizzle with honey. Sprinkle with chopped mint and top with grated cheese. Place under broiler until cheese melts and is lightly browned.

Greek mushrooms, cooked with vegetables, herbs and wine; excellent served warm as a vegetable or chilled as a salad

GREEK MUSHROOMS

2 medium carrots, coarsely chopped
1 medium onion, coarsely chopped
5 T olive oil
2 sprigs parsley, 2 sprigs thyme, 2 bay leaves and 1 stalk
    celery tied together
1 garlic clove, finely minced
½ cup dry white wine
2 medium tomatoes, peeled and chopped
4 cups small button mushrooms
1 t salt
¼ t freshly ground black pepper
¼ cup minced parsley

Sauté carrots and onion in 3 tablespoons olive oil until soft and golden. Add tied herbs, garlic and wine; simmer a few minutes. Add tomatoes and mushrooms; season with salt and pepper. Cook uncovered for 15 to 20 minutes stirring occasionally. Remove from heat and allow to cool. Remove herbs and add remaining 2 tablespoons olive oil. (Reheat to serve warm or chill to serve cold.) Sprinkle with minced parsley just before serving.

An interesting Bulgarian style of preparing green beans with eggs and yogurt; double recipe to serve as a main entree

GREEN BEANS AND EGGS WITH YOGURT

1 small onion, finely minced
2 T butter
1 T flour
½ t salt
¼ t freshly ground black pepper
⅛ t cayenne pepper
1 cup chopped cooked green beans
4 eggs, slightly beaten
½ cup plain yogurt
1 T chopped fresh dill

Sauté onion in butter until tender. Stir in flour, salt, black pepper and cayenne; add green beans and mix well. Stir in eggs; cook, stirring until almost set. Add yogurt and dill; continue to cook until set. Serve immediately.

Tomatoes Persillees are Spanish style tomato halves topped with pine nuts and minced parsley

TOMATOES TOPPED WITH PINE NUTS

2 large or 4 medium tomatoes
½ t salt
3 T olive oil
½ cup pine nuts
3 T butter
1 small garlic clove, finely minced
¾ cup minced parsley
¼ t black pepper

Halve tomatoes, sprinkle with salt and let drain for 30 minutes. In a skillet, sauté tomato halves in olive oil for 2 to 3 minutes on each side, or until they are just softened. Transfer, cut side up, to an ovenproof serving dish and keep warm in a 350° preheated oven. In the same skillet, sauté pine nuts in remaining olive oil for a few minutes, until they are lightly colored. Spoon into a small dish. Add butter to skillet; sauté garlic, parsley and black pepper, stirring constantly for 5 minutes or until butter is lightly colored. Spoon parsley mixture on the tomatoes and top with pine nuts. Serve immediately.

Kasha, a porridge made with buckwheat groats, is eaten in Russia as a staple part of the diet; with milk for breakfast, served as an accompaniment to other foods, or fried and served with melted butter or sour cream

KASHA

1 cup medium buckwheat groats (kasha)
1 egg, slightly beaten
1 t salt
2 cups boiling water
2 T butter

Combine buckwheat groats and egg in a saucepan; cook, stirring constantly, until grains are toasted and separate. Add salt and boiling water; cook slowly, tightly covered until grains are tender and liquid is absorbed, about 30 minutes. Stir in butter.

Light and delicate, Julienne De Carottes Au Gratin, carrots, cream and eggs in a superb French recipe.

CARROTS AU GRATIN

2 lbs. carrots, coarsely grated
⅓ cup butter
2 T lemon juice
1 t sugar
¾ t salt
⅛ t black pepper
1½ cups cream
3 eggs

Combine carrots, butter, lemon juice and sugar in a saucepan; pour over enough water to barely cover. Bring to a boil and simmer, covered, for 30 minutes. Over a high flame, cook, stirring constantly until liquid has evaporated. Add salt and pepper; cool for 10 minutes. Whisk together cream and eggs; stir into carrots. Pour into a buttered baking dish; bake in a 375° preheated oven until surface is swelled and brown, about 35 minutes. Serve immediately.

Mexican Quimbombo à la Criolla, is creole-style okra prepared with tomatoes, green peppers, onions and seasonings

OKRA CREOLE

1½ lbs. tender okra, cut into ½-inch slices
1 T wine vinegar
2 T olive oil
2 T butter
1 celery stalk, finely chopped
1 small onion, finely chopped
1 small green bell pepper, finely chopped
1 garlic clove, finely minced
½ t crushed oregano
½ t cumin
1 bay leaf
2 cups finely minced tomatoes
1 T lemon juice
1 t salt
¼ t freshly ground black pepper

Place okra in a bowl, cover with cold water; add vinegar and soak. In a large skillet heat oil and butter; add celery, onion and green pepper; sauté until transparent. Add garlic, oregano, cumin and bay leaf; mix well, cover and cook until vegetables are tender, about 5 minutes. Add tomatoes and cook 10 minutes. Drain okra and add to frying pan. Add lemon juice, salt and pepper; cover and cook at low heat until okra is tender, stirring occasionally. Taste for seasoning.

German Blumenkohl is cauliflower with a sauce of egg yolk and buttered bread crumbs

CAULIFLOWER WITH EGG SAUCE

1 head cauliflower, divided into medium-size flowerets
2 egg yolks
3 T butter
1 T bread crumbs

Cook cauliflower until tender. Remove cauliflower, without breaking sections, to a heated platter. Beat egg yolks and pour over cauliflower. In butter, lightly brown bread crumbs; spoon over cauliflower, serve immediately.

A flavorsome Swedish vegetable casserole combining leeks and tomatoes in a creamy sauce

TOMATO AND LEEKS

5 leeks, cut into 1-inch slices
2 T butter
4 medium tomatoes, sliced
2 eggs
2 t flour
1 cup milk
½ t salt
¼ t black pepper

In a frying pan, slowly sauté leeks in 1 tablespoon butter until tender; remove leeks to a dish. Add 1 tablespoon butter to frying pan and lightly sauté tomatoe slices. In a casserole dish arrange leeks and tomatoes. Beat eggs, flour, milk, salt and pepper together; pour over leeks and tomatoes. Bake in a 450° preheated oven for 30 minutes. Traditionally this is served with fried potatoes.

An Italian favorite, Melenzana Alla Parmigiana, eggplant with tomatoes and Mozzarella cheese

PARMESAN EGGPLANT

2 T tomato paste
2½ cups cooked tomatoes
6 T olive oil
1¼ t salt
1 medium eggplant, cut crosswise into ½-inch slices
2 cups dry bread crumbs
½ cup grated Parmesan cheese
1 T finely minced parsley
2 garlic cloves, finely minced
¼ t black pepper
½ lb. thinly sliced Mozzarella cheese

Blend tomato paste with tomatoes. Add 1 tablespoon olive oil and ¼ teaspoon salt; simmer in a saucepan for 30 minutes. Pour 5 tablespoons olive oil in a large frying pan. Fry eggplant slices in hot oil until soft and light brown, about 3 minutes on each side. Remove from pan and sprinkle each slice with remaining 1 teaspoon salt. Mix bread crumbs, Parmesan cheese, parsley, garlic and pepper. In a baking dish place one layer of eggplant; sprinkle with bread crumb mixture and pour some tomato sauce over. Alternate layers until all ingredients are used. Top with Mozzarella cheese. Bake in a 350° preheated oven for 25 minutes.

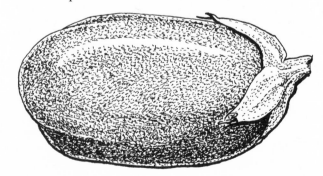

Traditionally made in the summer when fresh vegetables are bountiful, Tourlou, is a Turkish-Greek classic, cooked slowly while flavors gently intermingle

TOURLOU

6 T olive oil
4 medium tomatoes, peeled and chopped
1 small eggplant, sliced
2 medium zucchini, cut in 1-inch slices
2 small carrots, cut in diagonal slices
1 cup green beans, cut in 2-inch lengths
1 medium green bell pepper, sliced in rings
1 medium onion, thinly sliced
2 T chopped parsley
1 garlic clove, finely minced
1 t salt
¼ t black pepper
1 cup fresh lima beans

Pour oil in bottom of a Dutch oven. Layer vegetables in the following order; tomatoes, eggplant, zucchini, carrots, green beans, green pepper and onions. Combine parsley, garlic, salt and pepper; sprinkle over vegetables. Cover and cook over low heat about 1½-hours. Add lima beans and continue cooking until lima beans are tender, 30 to 40 minutes. Serve hot or cold. Will serve four as a main dish, or eight as a side dish or hors d' oeuvre.

Lovely pastry tarts filled with mushrooms and cream, from Switzerland

MUSHROOM-CREAM TARTS

Pastry for 2-crust pie
3 eggs, beaten
3 T dry white wine
2 T finely sliced green onions
1 small garlic clove, finely minced
½ t salt
⅛ t black pepper
⅛ t nutmeg
1½ cups cream
1½ cups sliced mushrooms

Prepare pastry and roll out, half at a time. Cut into 4-inch circles and line tart pans or large muffin cups. Brush pastry with beaten egg; reserve remaining eggs for filling mixture. Combine wine, green onions and garlic in a small saucepan. Bring to a boil, reduce heat and simmer 2 minutes. Cool. To beaten eggs add salt, pepper, nutmeg and cream; beat until well blended. Stir in wine mixture. Divide mushrooms among tart shells. Add about ¼ cup of egg-cream mixture to each. Place on baking sheet and bake in a 400° preheated oven for 15 to 20 minutes. Makes 12 to 14 tarts.

Here is nutritious Israeli Kash Varnitchkes; noodles and buckwheat groats cooked with onion

NOODLES WITH BUCKWHEAT GROATS

3 cups broad noodles
½ cup uncooked whole buckwheat groats (kasha)
1 cup finely chopped onion
3 T rendered chicken fat or butter
½ t salt
¼ t black pepper

Cook noodles in boiling water until tender, about 8 to 10 minutes; drain. Cook groats in 3 cups of boiling water for 10 to 12 minutes; drain. In a large skillet, cook onion in chicken fat until tender but not brown, about 5 minutes. Stir in noodles, groats, salt and pepper. Toss until well mixed. Taste for seasoning.

The Turkish enjoy savory Dolmas, green peppers stuffed with anchovies, olives, raisins and pine nuts

PEPPERS STUFFED WITH ANCHOVIES

4 small green bell peppers
6 anchovy fillets, cut into small pieces
12 pitted black olives, coarsely chopped
3 T raisins
2 T shelled pine nuts
2 T olive oil
¼ cup hot water

Cut a slice from stalk end of peppers to serve as a lid; remove seeds. Combine anchovies, olives, raisins and pine nuts. Stuff peppers and place pepper lids on top. Arrange peppers in a baking dish and drizzle tops with olive oil. Pour hot water around the peppers and bake in a 350° preheated oven for 45 minutes. Serve either hot or cool.

For a luncheon main dish serve Turkish spinach and eggs topped with yogurt

SPINACH AND EGGS WITH YOGURT

2 bunches spinach, chopped, cooked and drained
8 eggs
1½ cups plain yogurt
1 garlic clove, finely minced
½ cup grated Cheddar or Jack cheese
3 T finely minced parsley

Arrange spinach in a buttered shallow baking dish. Make 8 depressions in spinach with back of a spoon. Carefully break 1 egg into each depression. Combine yogurt, garlic and grated cheese; spoon over eggs. Place under a preheated broiler long enough for eggs to set and spinach to become hot and bubbly. Sprinkle with chopped parsley and serve immediately.

An ideal complement to chicken is Rödkål, a Norwegian recipe for red cabbage with apples and onions

RED CABBAGE

2 T butter
2 lbs. red cabbage, finely shredded
2 medium apples, peeled and sliced in wedges
1 medium onion, chopped
2 t caraway seed, slightly crushed
1 t salt
2 T maple syrup
4 T vinegar
2 T water

In a large heavy saucepan, melt butter. Add cabbage, apples, onion, caraway seeds, salt, syrup, vinegar and water. Cover and bring to a boil, stirring occasionally to blend. Reduce heat and simmer, stirring occasionally, until tender, about 45 minutes; add a little water if necessary.

Here is a delicate English corn pudding soufflé

CORN PUDDING SOUFFLÉ

4 eggs, beaten
2½ cups cream-style corn
⅛ t salt
¼ cup melted butter
4 T flour
3 t sugar
⅔ cup milk
3 t baking powder

Combine eggs, corn, salt, butter, flour, sugar and milk; add baking powder and mix well. Spoon into a buttered 1½-quart soufflé dish and bake in a 425° oven for 30 minutes. Serve immediately.

Ch'Ao Chieh Lan is Chinese stir-fried broccoli, crisp-textured and retaining a beautiful jade color

STIR-FRIED BROCCOLI

2 T peanut or corn oil
2 lbs. broccoli, separate flowerets, peel and cut stem only in 1½ × 1½-inch pieces
1 t salt
1 t sugar
4 T water
1 T cornstarch

In a wok or large frying pan heat oil and stir-fry broccoli for about 2 minutes. Add salt and sugar, mixing well. Add 2 tablespoons water and cover. Cook over high heat for 2 minutes, stirring once. Combine cornstarch and 2 tablespoons water, add to broccoli and stir-fry one more minute. Taste for seasoning; serve immediately.

Note: Asparagus, zucchini or cauliflower cut into 1-inch pieces may be prepared in the same manner.

A favorite among Albanians is Dolma me Vaj, green peppers stuffed with rice, pine nuts, tomatoes and seasonings

STUFFED GREEN PEPPERS

4 large green bell peppers
1 small onion, finely chopped
2 garlic cloves, finely minced
½ cup olive oil
1 cup uncooked rice
½ cup coarsely chopped pine nuts
2 medium tomatoes, peeled and chopped
2 T lemon juice
⅛ t cayenne pepper
1 t salt
¼ t black pepper
⅓ cup chopped parsley

Cut tops from pepper and scoop out seeds. Sauté onion and garlic in oil until tender. Add rice and pine nuts; sauté for several minutes until rice becomes translucent. Add tomatoes, lemon juice, cayenne, salt and black pepper; cook slowly, stirring frequently, for 10 minutes. Add parsley and mix well. Taste for seasoning. Spoon into peppers, filling loosely. Arrange in heavy saucepan so that peppers fit closely together. Add boiling water to half cover peppers. Cook slowly, tightly covered, until rice filling is cooked, about 1 hour. May be served hot or cold.

Crookneck squash, green onions, and celery combined and seasoned with lemon in a delicious French style

SQUASH AMANDINE

2 T butter
3 T slivered almonds
4 green onions, cut into ½-inch pieces
½ cup diagonally sliced celery
1 lb. crookneck squash, cut into cubes
½ t salt
1 t grated lemon peel
1 T lemon juice

Melt butter in a large skillet; add almonds and stir over high heat until golden. Remove from pan and reserve. Add onions, celery and squash; stir-fry over high heat for 1 minute. Add salt, lemon peel and juice. Reduce heat to medium, cover and cook until squash is just tender, about 5 minutes. Stir in almonds and serve at once.

Spanish Arroz con Azafrán is a saffron rice; an excellent accompaniment for chicken or seafood

SAFFRON RICE

2 T olive oil
2 T finely chopped onions
1 cup uncooked long-grain rice
2 cups boiling water
1 t salt
⅛ t saffron

In a heavy skillet, heat olive oil; add onions, cook and stir until soft but not brown, about 5 minutes. Add rice and stir for a few minutes to coat grains well with oil. Add water, salt and saffron, bring to a boil, stirring constantly. Cover pan tightly and reduce heat to low. Simmer until all the liquid has been absorbed by the rice, about 20 minutes. Let stand 10 minutes. Fluff rice with a fork before serving.

Zanahorias Natas, is a simple and subtle Mexican preparation of carrots and sour cream

CARROTS IN SOUR CREAM

10 young carrots, cut in jullienne strips
1 T butter
¼ t salt
1 cup sour cream
1 T chopped chives

Sauté carrots slowly in butter until tender. Add salt and sour cream; heat, stirring gently over low flame. Spoon into a serving dish and sprinkle with chives.

Indonesian Gado Gado, is sautéed spinach and bean sprouts with a peanut sauce

SPINACH AND BEAN SPROUTS WITH PEANUT SAUCE

2 T oil
4 cups bean sprouts
1 green onion, finely sliced
1 bunch spinach, torn into pieces and drained well
½ cup peanut butter
1 t sugar
¼ t fresh grated ginger

In a skillet, heat oil, add bean sprouts, onion and spinach; sauté lightly, just enough to wilt vegetables. In a saucepan mix peanut butter, sugar and ginger; heat very slowly to prevent burning. Spoon vegetables into a serving dish and pour peanut sauce over. Serve immediately.

Fritada De Espanaca is a delicious Italian spinach pie made with eggs and cheese

SPINACH PIE

1 bunch spinach, cut in small pieces, cooked and drained
2 eggs, beaten
4 T cottage cheese
2 T grated Romano cheese
1 medium boiled potato, mashed
½ t salt
4 T olive oil

Blend together spinach, eggs, cottage cheese, Romano cheese, potato and salt. Slightly heat oil in an 8-inch pie pan; add mixture and bake in a 350° preheated oven for 10 minutes. Serve immediately, sliced into wedges.

Indian Pullao is a curried rice garnished with egg slices, raisins and almonds

CURRIED RICE

1 large onion, sliced
1½ T butter
2-inch stick of cinnamon
2 whole cloves
2 whole cardamon pods, cracked
1 bay leaf
½ t salt
¼ t turmeric
1 cup uncooked long-grain rice
2 cups water
1 hard-boiled egg, sliced
⅓ cup raisins
¼ cup toasted slivered almonds

In a saucepan, sauté onions in butter until tender but not brown. Add cinnamon, cloves, cardamom, bay leaf, salt, turmeric and rice; cook and stir 5 minutes, but do not brown. Stir in water, bring to a boil; reduce heat; cover and cook for 20 minutes. Remove from heat and let stand 10 minutes. Fluff with a fork and spoon onto a serving platter. Garnish with egg slices, raisins and almonds.

A tropical rice taste sensation; rice cooked with orange juice is an excellent accompaniment to chicken

ORANGE RICE

1 cup diagonally sliced celery
4 T finely minced onion
4 T butter
1½ cups water
1 cup orange juice
1½ T grated orange rind
1¼ t salt
1 cup uncooked rice
1 small orange, peeled and sectioned

In a skillet, sauté celery and onion in butter until just tender. Stir in water, orange juice, orange rind, salt and rice; cover, reduce heat to low and cook for 30 minutes. Turn heat off and let stand covered for 10 minutes. Spoon onto a serving dish and top with orange sections.

Here is a delicious cheese-stuffed eggplant we enjoyed for lunch in a New Orleans restaurant

CHEESE STUFFED EGGPLANT

2 small eggplants, halved lengthwise and pulp removed
    leavng a ½-inch thick shell
1 medium onion, chopped
2 garlic cloves, finely minced
3 T butter
3 T oil
½ cup minced parsley
1 t salt
½ t thyme
½ t oregano
5 T grated Parmesan cheese
2½ cups grated Jack cheese
2 large tomatoes, chopped
Parsley sprigs

In a skillet, sauté chopped eggplant pulp, onion and garlic in butter and oil until eggplant is tender, about 10 minutes. Stir in parsley, salt, thyme, oregano, Parmesan cheese, 2 cups Jack cheese and tomatoes. Spoon stuffing into eggplant shells; place in a baking pan and sprinkle with remaining Jack cheese. Bake in a 400° preheated oven for 25 minutes. With a spatula carefully remove to a warmed platter and garnish with parsley sprigs.

Here's a recipe created on our return from Egypt; a spinach crust filled with whole button mushrooms, cream and cheese garnished with buttered almonds

BAKED MUSHROOMS IN A SPINACH CRUST

2 cups cooked leaf spinach
4 cups small button mushrooms
1 cup cream
1 cup grated sharp Cheddar cheese
1 T grated onion
1 t salt
¼ t dry mustard
¼ t paprika
3 T slivered sautéed almonds
1 T finely minced parsley

Line a 9-inch glass pie pan with spinach. Cover with mushrooms, stem side down. Combine cream, cheese, onion, salt and dry mustard; pour over mushrooms. Bake in a 350° preheated oven for 30 minutes. Remove from oven; sprinkle with paprika, almonds and parsley; serve immediately.

A hearty vegetable dish is Turkish Nivik; garbanzo beans, spinach and seasonings slowly simmered together

GARBANZO BEANS AND SPINACH

1 medium onion, finely chopped
6 T butter
2 bunches of spinach, coarsely chopped
3 T tomato paste
1 cup water
2 cups cooked garbanzo beans
1 t salt
¼ t black pepper
⅛ t cayenne pepper

In a heavy saucepan sauté onion in butter for a few minutes. Add spinach and cook, stirring constantly, until leaves are wilted. Dissolve tomato paste in water and add to spinach along with garbanzo beans, salt, black pepper and cayenne pepper; mix throughly. Cover and simmer slowly for 1 hour; add more water if necessary. Especially good made early in the day and reheated just before serving.

Occasionally one has the time and desire for the taste of homemade noodles

HOMEMADE NOODLES

3 egg yolks
1 egg
3 T cold water
1 t salt
2 cups flour

Beat egg yolks and egg until very light. Beat in cold water and salt. With hands, thoroughly mix in flour. Divide dough into 3 parts. Roll dough, 1 part at a time, into paper-thin rectangles, on a lightly floured cloth covered board. Place between 2 dish towels until dough is partially dry. Roll rectangle around rolling pin; slip out rolling pin. With a thin sharp knife cut into ½-inch strips. Shake out strips and allow to dry, about 2 hours, before using or storing. Makes 6 cups uncooked noodles.

To Cook

Add 1 tablespoon salt to 3 quarts rapidly boiling water. Drop in noodles; cook uncovered, stirring occasionally with a fork to prevent sticking. Cook until just tender, about 8 to 10 minutes. Drain immediately in a colander.

One of the most delicate pastas I ever tasted was Fettucini in Rome; egg noodles, butter and Parmesan cheese gently mixed together

FETTUCINI

4 cups uncooked broad egg noodles
¾ cup heavy cream
1 cup fresh butter
½ lb. freshly grated Parmesan cheese
Freshly ground black pepper

Cook noodles in boiling, salted water until tender, about 10 minutes; drain. Place noodles in a warm bowl, add cream and chunks of butter. Mix thoroughly by constantly turning the noodles rather than tossing them. Fold in cheese until all the noodles are thoroughly coated. Season with pepper and serve immediately from the bowl.

Many of the recipes in this cookbook suggest serving rice as an accompaniment; one is plain rice, the other is rice pilaf, an Armenian recipe that goes well with any of the Middle east foods

PLAIN RICE

2 cups water
½ t salt
1 T butter or oil
1 cup long grain white rice

Bring water to a boil; add salt and butter. Stir in rice with a fork. Reduce heat to low; cover tightly and steam 20-25 minutes. Makes 3 cups.

RICE PILAF

2 cups chicken broth
4 T butter
½ t salt
1 cup long-grain white rice
¼ t black pepper

In a saucepan, bring chicken broth to a boil; add butter and salt. Pour in rice and stir gently with a fork. Lower heat; cover and cook until all moisture is absorbed and the grains are tender, about 25 minutes. Remove from heat. Mix and fluff gently with a fork; sprinkle with pepper. Cover and let steam 15 minutes. Makes 3 cups.

A hearty vegetable loaf made with walnuts, carrots and cheese; California style

CARROT-NUT LOAF

1 large onion, chopped
1 large green bell pepper, finely chopped
1 cup shredded carrots
⅔ cup chopped walnuts
1 egg
¼ cup brown rice flour (or whole-wheat flour)
1¼ cups whole-wheat soft bread crumbs
½ t basil
¼ cup milk
1 cup grated Cheddar cheese

Combine onion, pepper, carrots, nuts, egg, flour, bread crumbs, basil and milk; mix throughly. Turn into an oiled 8-inch loaf pan and bake in a 325° preheated oven for 45 minutes. Just before serving, sprinkle cheese over top of loaf; continue baking until cheese melts.

Here is Céleris à la Bonne Femme; a French style combination of celery, onion, carrot and tomato cooked in chicken broth

SAUTÉED CELERY

1 medium bunch celery
4 T chopped onion
1 medium carrot, grated
⅓ cup chicken broth
1 cup peeled and diced tomatoes
1 bay leaf
½ t salt
Few grindings fresh ground black pepper
2 T minced parsley

Trim off celery leaves and cut bunch in half lengthwise and then across in 2-inch pieces. In a saucepan, sauté onions and carrot in butter until browned. Mix in the celery and cook 3 minutes, stirring frequently. Add chicken broth, tomatoes, bay leaf, salt and black pepper. Cover and simmer 35 minutes over low heat. Discard bay leaf, taste for seasoning. Spoon into serving dish and sprinkle with parsley.

While in Moscow we enjoyed this Russian recipe, a combination of mushrooms and onions in sour cream

MUSHROOMS AND SOUR CREAM

½ cup finely minced onion
3 T butter
4 cups sliced mushrooms
1 t salt
¼ t black pepper
½ t minced dillweed
1½ t paprika
¾ cup sour cream

In a skillet, sauté onion in butter for 5 minutes. Add mushrooms, salt, pepper and dillweed; cook until browned and liquid is absorbed. Blend in paprika and sour cream. Heat, do not allow to boil; serve immediately.

The Italians cook a delicious combination of eggplant, tomatoes and cheese; excellent served as a vegetable or luncheon main dish

EGGPLANT AND RICOTTA CHEESE

1 eggplant, cut in thin slices
1½ cups cooked plum tomatoes
1 cup water
3 T olive oil
1 t salt
¼ t black pepper
1 cup Ricotta cheese

Soak eggplant in salted water for 5 minutes; drain dry. Combine tomatoes, water and olive oil in a saucepan; bring to a boil, add salt and pepper. Add eggplant and simmer over low heat for 30 minutes. Gently spoon into a baking dish and top with spoonfuls of cheese. Bake in a 350° preheated oven for 15 minutes.

An easy-to-make, old-country recipe is Epinards en Masse from France; spinach cooked in seasoned sour cream

SPINACH WITH SOUR CREAM

1 cup chopped onion
1 garlic clove, finely minced
2 T butter
1 bunch of spinach, chopped
1 T chopped parsley
2 T bread crumbs
2 T grated Parmesan cheese
1 cup sour cream

Sauté onion and garlic in the butter until tender but not browned. Add the spinach and sauté for 5 minutes, stirring occasionally. Add parsley, bread crumbs and Parmesan cheese; mix well and cook over low heat another 5 minutes. Fold in sour cream and heat. Serve at once.

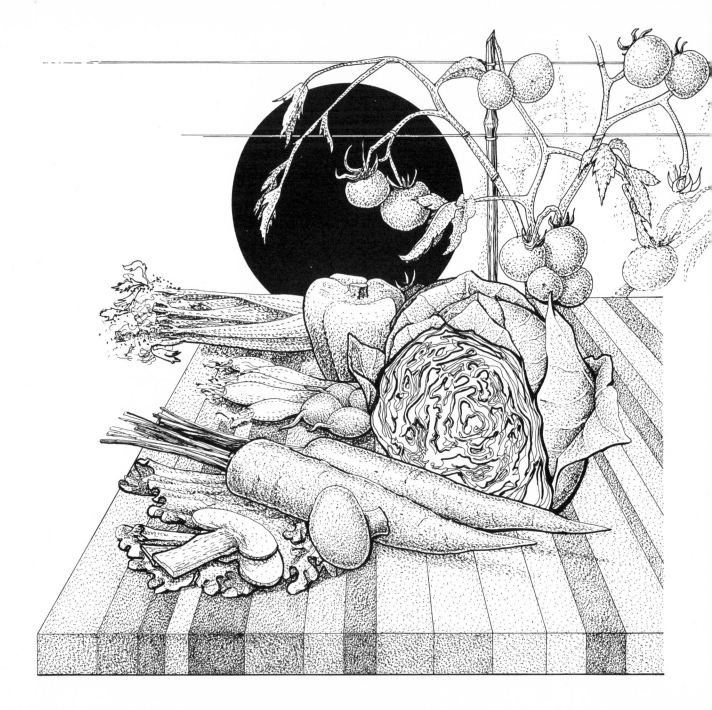

salads

A salad is one of the most versatile foods a cook can prepare. It can be served as an appetizer, a side dish, or hearty enough to be a meal in itself for warm weather dining. With our increased awareness of the importance of fruits and vegetables in a basic diet, salads of all types have become firmly established in our daily meals. Aside from the traditional crisp green salad, spark the meal occasionally with variety and new taste sensations. In many parts of the world, yogurt is combined with vegetables to create an unusual, healthful and cooling salad. In the Middle East, eggplant (rich in minerals and vitamins) is prepared in many tasty varieties. Legumes and grains made into salads offer tantalizing textures and flavors. Armenians traditionally serve with their main entree a large platter of fresh cut vegetables, such as lettuce wedges, celery and carrot sticks, cucumber slices, radishes, green onions and watercress. Raw vegetables and fruits contain the natural cellulose or bulk our bodies need. Some fresh raw food should be eaten daily to contribute necessary fibrous roughage. Whatever the salad choice may be, it should be served on thoroughly chilled plates and garnished with maximum eye appeal. Through the salad selection as with vegetables and grains achieve an interesting contrast of flavor, texture and color in your meals, while assuring a proper vitamin and mineral balance.

Salads

Piyaz, a Turkish salad made with dried white beans

WHITE BEAN SALAD

1 cup dried large white beans
4 T olive oil
4 T lemon juice
4 green onions, thinly sliced
1 T dill weed
1 T fresh mint leaves
Salt
Black pepper
1 medium tomato, cubed
1 hard-boiled egg, sliced
1 T chopped parsley

Cover beans with water and bring to a boil; reduce heat and cook for 2 minutes. Remove beans from heat and let stand for 1 hour. Reheat beans to boiling; reduce heat and cook until tender, about 1½ hours. Add water if necessary during cooking. In a bowl, combine well drained beans, oil, lemon juice, green onions, dill, mint, salt and pepper to taste. Marinate for at least 1 hour. Gently mix in tomato; spoon salad onto a serving platter. Decorate with egg slices and sprinkle with parsley.

A delicious salad that can also be served as an appetizer is Bulgarian Zelen Haviar. Eggplant with tomatoes and bell pepper; seasoned with garlic, olive oil and lemon juice

EGGPLANT SALAD

1 large eggplant
2 medium green bell peppers, minced
2 medium tomatoes, minced
2 garlic cloves, crushed
1 small yellow chili pepper, minced
4 T olive oil
4 T lemon juice
4 T chopped fresh parsley
1 t salt
Freshly ground black pepper

Prick eggplant in several places; cook on a cookie sheet in a 400° preheated oven until soft, about 50 minutes. Remove and discard skin; chop pulp with a knife and in a bowl mix well with remaining ingredients. Chill thoroughly. As an appetizer serve with crusty bread or crackers. As a salad mound on lettuce leaves on individual plates.

A welcome change of pace from a green salad, try these French marinated anise carrots

ANISE CARROT SALAD

8 medium carrots, diagonally cut into ½ inch slices
6 T olive oil
4 T lemon juice
1 T anise seeds
1 T white vinegar
¼ t black pepper
½ t salt
Lettuce leaves

Cook carrots until crisp-tender; run under cold water to stop cooking process. Combine olive oil, lemon juice, anise seeds, vinegar, pepper and salt. Pour over drained carrots. Cover and refrigerate overnight. Just before serving arrange lettuce leaves on plates and spoon on carrots.

Caponata, a Sicilian salad made with eggplant, olives, tomatoes and pine nuts is a basic favorite

EGGPLANT AND OLIVE SALAD

2 medium eggplants, pared and diced into 1-inch cubes
2 t salt
8 T olive oil
1 large red onion, sliced lengthwise
2 celery stalks, thinly sliced
1¾ cups Italian style tomatoes, undrained
¾ cup pitted black olives, cut into wedges
2 T capers
1 t sugar
¼ cup wine vinegar
½ t coarsely ground black pepper
Shredded iceberg lettuce
4 T pine nuts

Sprinkle eggplant with 1 teaspoon salt. In a skillet, heat half of the oil; sauté eggplant until lightly browned and remove to a large bowl. Add remaining oil to the skillet, heat; add onion, celery, tomatoes and remaining salt. Cook until onion and celery are tender, about 5 minutes; combine with eggplant. Add olives, capers, sugar, vinegar and pepper. Chill several hours. Serve on lettuce and top with pine nuts.

Beans and lentils make a nourishing salad which the Egyptians call Fool Midammis

BEAN AND LENTIL SALAD

1 cup dried small fava or broad beans
1 T dried lentils
4 cups water
4 T olive oil
1 T lemon juice
½ t salt
3 T finely chopped parsley
8 pitted black olives, preferably Mediterranean type

Wash beans and lentils thoroughly. In a heavy saucepan bring water to a boil; add beans and lentils, reduce heat to low and partially cover. Simmer until beans are tender, about 3 to 4 hours; check occasionally to make sure beans stay moist, add a few tablespoons of water if necessary. When beans are done there should be almost no liquid left in the pan. Transfer contents of the pan to a bowl and cool to room temperature. With a whisk or fork, beat oil, lemon juice and salt together in a deep bowl. Add beans and lentils mashing them gently with a fork; stir until most of the dressing is absorbed. To serve, spread the bean mixture on a platter; sprinkle with parsley and garnish with olives.

Here is a simple-to-prepare Hungarian salad, Paprika Salata. Green pepper strips sautéed in oil.

GREEN PEPPER SALAD

4 large green bell peppers, cut into 1-inch strips
4 T vegetable oil
3 T vinegar
1 medium onion, minced
4 T chopped fresh parsley
Salt
Black pepper

Sauté bell pepper in oil until tender. In a bowl, gently mix together; bell pepper, vinegar, onion and parsley. Season to taste with salt and pepper. Cover and chill for 24 hours.

A different type of Mexican salad made with radishes and avocados

AVOCADO AND RADISH SALAD

16 firm white or red radishes, thinly sliced
½ t salt
1 t minced onion
½ t chopped chives
1 T minced parsley
¼ t freshly ground black pepper
2 T lemon juice
2 ripe avocados, peeled and halved
Lettuce leaves

Sprinkle radish slices with salt and chill in the refrigerator for 30 minutes. Combine onions, chives, parsley, pepper and lemon juice. Drain excess water off radishes; add to mixture and toss well. Arrange avocado halves on a bed of lettuce leaves and fill with radish mixture.

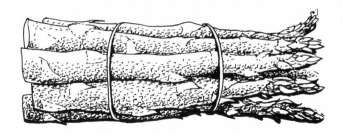

Delicate molded salads contribute beauty and variety to the Swedish smorgasbord; here is one made with asparagus, tomatoes and lemon gelatin

ASPARAGUS LEMON MOLD

6 whole stalks cooked asparagus
2 cups boiling water
6 ounces lemon-flavored gelatin
1½ cups cold water
2 T vinegar
½ cup mayonnaise
½ t salt
1 cup cooked diced asparagus
1 cup diced tomatoes
1 T chopped parsley
Dash of chervil
Lettuce leaves
Lemon slices

Arrange whole stalks of asparagus diagonally in a 9×5-inch loaf pan. Pour boiling water over gelatin in a bowl; stir until gelatin is dissolved. Mix 1 cup dissolved gelatin with 1 cup cold water; gently pour over asparagus and chill until set. Mix remaining 1 cup hot gelatin with ½ cup cold water, vinegar, mayonnaise and salt; blend with a rotary beater until smooth. Chill in the freezer, about 25 minutes; whip until fluffy and thick. Fold in diced asparagus, tomatoes, parsley and chervil; pour over clear gelatin-asparagus layer. Chill until firm. Unmold and garnish with lettuce leaves and lemon slices.

Indian onion Raitha will appeal to those who enjoy yogurt and onions

YOGURT AND ONIONS

2 cups plain yogurt
2 T lemon juice
½ t salt
⅛ t black pepper
1 large onion, peeled and thinly sliced

Combine yogurt, lemon juice, salt and pepper in a bowl; stir in onion slices, separated into rings. Cover and chill at least 3 hours.

Finnish cabbage and apple salad, an interesting change from traditional salads

CABBAGE AND APPLE SALAD

3 cups shredded cabbage
2 medium unpeeled apples, shredded
½ cup sour cream
1 t sugar
⅓ cup orange juice

Combine cabbage and apples. Mix sour cream, sugar and orange juice; pour over salad. Serve chilled.

This is a most unusual Yugoslavian salad, a combination of cucumbers and walnuts; also makes an excellent appetizer served on slices of dark bread

CUCUMBER AND WALNUT SALAD

1 T wine vinegar
1 garlic clove, crushed

4 T olive oil
2 cups peeled, diced cucumbers
½ cup finely chopped walnuts
Salt
Freshly ground black pepper
Crisp lettuce leaves
Chopped fresh mint

Combine vinegar, garlic and olive oil in a bowl; add cucumbers and walnuts, mix well. Season to taste with salt and pepper. Chill thoroughly. Spoon mixture onto lettuce leaves; traditionally garnished with chopped fresh mint.

A low calorie mushroom and celery combination enhanced with a nutritious olive oil dressing is a very popular California salad

MUSHROOM AND CELERY SALAD

3 cups thinly sliced fresh mushrooms
1 cup diced celery
½ cup diced green bell pepper
½ cup diced red onion
½ cup diced pimentos

In a bowl, combine mushrooms, celery, pepper, onion and pimentos. Toss salad with olive oil dressing.

Olive Oil Dressing

3 T red wine vinegar
1 t minced garlic clove
1 t Worcestershire sauce
1 t salt
6 T olive oil

In a small bowl, combine vinegar, garlic, Worcestershire sauce and salt: add olive oil in a stream, whisking to blend.

Chinese prepare mung bean sprouts with egg strips and soy sauce to make a crunchy salad

MUNG BEAN SPROUTS SALAD

4 cups fresh mung bean sprouts
1 T sesame seed or vegetable oil
1 egg, beaten
¼ cup scallion, green part only

Remove green skin from bean sprouts (by stirring with hands in a large basin of cold water) and drain. Heat oil in a large frying pan; pour in beaten egg, swirl pan quickly so egg covers entire surface, cook until set. When egg has cooled, slice into julienne strips and set aside in a small bowl. Shortly before serving prepare soy sauce dressing. Add mung beans, scallions and egg strips to dressing and toss.

Soy Sauce Dressing

¼ cup wine vinegar
2 T soy sauce
4 T sesame seed or vegetable oil
½ t sugar
½ t hot pepper sauce

Thoroughly mix all ingredients in a salad bowl.

Jicama, a popular Mexican root vegetable that is sweet and crunchy; combined here with cucumber and orange cubes

JICAMA SALAD

1 cup jicama, pared and cubed
1 small cucumber, sliced
1 small orange, peeled and cubed
1½ T lemon juice
½ t chili powder
¼ t salt

Combine jicama, cucumber and orange in a serving bowl. Sprinkle with lemon juice and chili powder; toss thoroughly. Cover and chill a couple of hours. Just before serving, add salt and toss again.

South Africans enjoy green bean Atjar, beans pickled in spiced oil, hot and delicious

STRING BEANS IN SPICED OIL

2 lbs. fresh green string beans, cut lengthwise into quarters
Boiling water
2 T salt
1 cup vegetable oil
2 T curry powder
2 t ground turmeric
2 T finely chopped, fresh hot yellow chilies
1½ T finely chopped garlic
1 t fenugreek seeds, coarsely crushed

Cover beans completely with boiling water and let stand for 2 minutes. Drain beans in a sieve and run cold water over to set color. Place beans in a bowl; add salt, stirring until dissolved. Cover tightly and let set at room temperature for a couple of hours. Drain, pressing out remaining liquid; place in a glass or ceramic bowl. In a small skillet, heat ¼ cup oil; add curry powder and turmeric, stir well. Add chilies, garlic and fenugreek; stirring constantly, pour in remaining oil, cook until mixture begins to splutter. Reduce heat and simmer for a few minutes; remove from heat and cool for about 1 hour. Pour oil mixture over beans and refrigerate, uncovered to pickle for 2 to 3 days before serving.

Namasu is one type of Japanese salad; paper-thin slices of cucumber and abalone with a vinegar sauce

FISH SALAD

*2 cucumbers, halved lengthwise and sliced into thin
    diagonal pieces*
½ t salt
¼ cup white vinegar
½ t monosodium glutamate
1 T sugar
½ cup abalone, sliced into thin strips
1 T abalone juice

Sprinkle cucumber slices lightly with salt, let set for 15 minutes; drain, pressing out remaining liquid. Combine vinegar, monosodium glutamate and sugar; mix with cucumber slices. Add abalone strips and abalone juice; mix thoroughly. Chill before serving.

The Russians prepare an unusual salad with sliced red radishes, hard-boiled eggs and sour cream

RADISH SALAD

2 hard-boiled eggs
1 cup sour cream
Salt
Black pepper
2 cups sliced red radishes
2 T minced parsley

Cut peeled eggs in half. Slip out yolks; mash with fork and combine with sour cream. Season with salt and pepper to taste. Spoon mixture over radishes on a serving plate; sprinkle with minced egg whites and parsley. Chill before serving.

This fruit salad has an Oriental flavor; fruit cocktail combined with bean sprouts, water chestnuts and a delicious dressing

ORIENTAL FRUIT SALAD

3½ cups fruit cocktail, drained
½ cup bean sprouts
½ cup thinly sliced water chestnuts
½ lettuce head, shredded

In a serving bowl, combine fruit cocktail, bean sprouts, water chestnuts and lettuce. Toss with fruit salad dressing.

Fruit Salad Dressing

½ cup sour cream
1 T mayonnaise
2 T lemon juice
2 t soy sauce
¼ cup finely sliced green onion
2 T chopped parsley
1 T finely chopped gingerroot
¼ t ground coriander

Thoroughly mix all ingredients and refrigerate until ready to serve salad.

A zesty Lebanese spinach salad made with spinach, bulgur, onions and oil

SPINACH-BULGUR SALAD

½ cup fine bulgur (cracked wheat)
1 cup cold water
1 medium onion, finely chopped
⅓ cup olive oil
1 bunch spinach, finely chopped
Salt
2 lemons, cut into wedges

Soak bulgur in cold water and set aside. In a skillet, sauté onion in heated oil until soft. Add spinach, cook and stir until tender, about 5 minutes; salt to taste and remove from heat. Drain bulgur and add to spinach; stir until well mixed. Spoon into a bowl and chill. Serve with lemon wedges to squeeze over salad before eating.

Yogurt, swiss chard and parsley combine to make a nourishing Armenian salad, Zadig Aghtzan

YOGURT AND SWISS CHARD SALAD

2 bunches swiss chard (only green leaves) coarsely chopped
3 cups plain yogurt
¾ cup finely chopped parsley
1 garlic clove, finely minced
1¼ t salt

Cook swiss chard until wilted; drain in a collander, when cooled, press out remaining liquid. In a bowl, combine swiss chard, yogurt, parsley, garlic and salt; mix thoroughly. Chill before serving.

Sweet and sour bean sprouts prepared Chinese style make a vitamin-rich, low calorie and inexpensive salad

SWEET AND SOUR BEAN SPROUTS

1 lb. fresh bean sprouts
3 T sugar
2 cups water
⅓ cup red wine vinegar
2 T olive oil
1 T soy sauce

Bring sprouts, 1 tablespoon sugar and water to a boil; cook 1 minute. Drain sprouts thoroughly and place in a shallow bowl. Stir in vinegar, olive oil, soy sauce and remaining sugar. Marinate bean sprouts for at least 12 hours; stirring gently from time to time. The mixture will keep several weeks under refrigeration.

Kolokithakia Me Yiaourto Salata, a unique Greek salad of zucchini and yogurt

YOGURT ZUCCHINI SALAD

1½ lbs. zucchini, cut into ½ inch slices
Olive oil
Salt
Black Pepper
2 garlic cloves, finely minced
1 cup plain yogurt
2 T lemon juice
Tomato wedges

Sauté zucchini in oil until barely tender and lightly browned on both sides; season lightly with salt and pepper, drain on paper towels and chill. Blend together garlic and yogurt; stir in lemon juice. Arrange chilled zucchini on a plate and pour yogurt sauce over. Garnish with tomato wedges.

Ensalada Mixta is a unique salad from South America that is made with avocado, cucumber, banana and bell pepper

AVOCADO-CUCUMBER-BANANA SALAD

1 medium avocado, peeled and sliced
1 medium cucumber, pared, halved and thinly sliced
2 medium bananas, peeled and sliced
½ medium green bell pepper, cut into thin strips
¼ cup sliced pimentos
¼ small onion, thinly sliced and separated into rings

Combine avocado, cucumber, bananas, pepper, pimento and onion in a salad bowl. Pour dressing over salad and marinate in the refrigerator for 1 hour. Gently toss salad before serving.

Dressing

4 T vinegar
3 T oil
½ t salt
Dash of hot pepper sauce

Combine all ingredients in a jar; cover and shake.

Lolig Bulgur Aghtzan is an Armenian recipe that is a unique, nutritious salad

TOMATO AND BULGUR SALAD

1 cup fine bulgur (cracked wheat)
2 ripe medium tomatoes, finely chopped
3 T tomato paste
4 T lemon juice
1 cup hot water
1 medium onion, finely chopped
6 T olive oil

⅛ t cayenne pepper
Salt to taste
4 T finely minced parsley

In a bowl mix together bulgur and tomatoes. Combine tomato paste, lemon juice and hot water; stir into bulgur mixture and let stand 1 hour. Sauté the onion in olive oil until tender; add to salad. Season with cayenne pepper and salt. Pile salad on a serving platter and sprinkle with parsley.

Spinach, apple and cucumber salad tossed with a mint dressing and sprinkled with sunflower seeds

SPINACH-APPLE SALAD

1 apple, cored and sliced
1 T lemon juice
1 bunch spinach, torn into bite-size pieces
1 small cucumber, peeled and sliced
¼ cup sliced radishes
4 T sunflower seeds

Sprinkle apple with lemon juice. In a bowl, combine spinach, cucumber, radishes and apple. Toss salad with mint dressing and sprinkle with sunflower seeds.

Mint Dressing

½ cup oil
2 T lemon juice
2 t chopped green onions
1 T chopped fresh mint or ½ t dried mint flakes
½ t salt
1 t sugar

Combine all ingredients in a small jar; cover and shake well. Makes ⅔ cup dressing.

While traveling in the U.S.S.R. we enjoyed this refreshing salad of beets and mushrooms in the Ukraine

BEET AND MUSHROOM SALAD

2 cups jullienne strips cooked beets
2 cups jullienne strips fresh mushrooms
1 small onion, thinly sliced and separated into rings

Combine beets, mushrooms and onion in a salad bowl. Toss salad with dressing and serve immediately.

Dressing

2 T vinegar
5 T oil
½ t sugar
¼ t salt
Dash of freshly ground black pepper

Combine all ingredients in a jar; cover and shake.

Osunomono is a simple oriental salad, made with cucumbers, shrimp and a vinegar-soy sauce dressing

CUCUMBER AND SHRIMP SALAD

2 large cucumbers
2 t salt
1 cup cooked tiny shrimp

Pare cucumbers lengthwise, leaving a few strips of green. Slice cucumbers very thin and place in a colander; sprinkle with salt and let stand for a few minutes. Mix with hands and squeeze out as much liquid as possible; transfer cucumbers to a salad bowl and mix in dressing. Cover and chill salad 1 to 2 hours. Mix in shrimp just before serving.

Dressing

4 T rice vinegar
1 T sugar
1 T soy sauce

Combine all ingredients in a jar; cover and shake.

A delicious recipe we first tasted in Bermuda; oyster salad on lettuce leaves, garnished with lemon slices

OYSTER SALAD

2 cups shucked oysters, and their liquid
2 cups chopped celery
Crisp lettuce leaves
8 lemon slices
8 parsley sprigs

Simmer oysters with liquid until edges curl; cool and drain. Cut each oyster into quarters. Toss with celery and enough French dressing to moisten. Arrange lettuce leaves on individual salad plates and spoon on oyster salad. Garnish with lemon slices and parsley.

French Dressing

1 cup olive oil
¼ cup vinegar
½ t salt
Dash of cayenne pepper
¼ t black pepper
2 T minced parsley

Combine all ingredients in a jar; cover and shake.

Lebanese Tabuli, a popular appetizer that may also be served as a salad, is made by combining bulgar, tomatoes, parsley and mint; which you eat by scooping up into crisp Romaine lettuce leaves

TABULI

1 cup fine bulgar (cracked wheat)
1 cup hot water
3 medium tomatoes, finely chopped
2 cups finely minced parsley
½ cup finely minced fresh mint
1 medium onion, finely minced
½ cup lemon juice
½ cup olive oil
1 t salt
¼ t black pepper
⅛ t allspice
⅛ t cayenne pepper
Crisp Romaine lettuce leaves

Combine bulgur and hot water in a large bowl; let stand 1 hour. Add tomatoes, parsley, mint and onion to bulgur. Sprinkle with lemon juice, olive oil, salt, black pepper, allspice and cayenne pepper; toss throughly. Taste for seasoning, add salt or additional cayenne pepper if desired. Pile mixture on a serving platter and surround with lettuce leaves.

breads

No perfume can compete with the fragrance of bread loaves baking and cooling. With the ever-growing return to cooking from scratch, home-baked yeast breads rank high on the list of foods that are popular with today's cooks. For most people of the world bread is cherished as the staff of life, the mainstay of their diet. When whole grains are used, bread is an inexpensive source of carbohydrates and vegetable proteins. In many American Indian tribes, the name for corn means "our mother," or "our life," or "she who sustains us." Their breads, made of corn, were either fried over an open fire or baked in thick-walled, beehive-shaped adobe ovens called *hornos*. Corn is also the basis of the popular tortilla of Mexico. Millet is made into *injera*, a thin soft bread of Africa. Rye is the basis of Russia's hearty, coarse bread and the dry, flat disk breads of the Scandinavian countries. Wheat is used in the peda and pocket bread of the Middle East as well as in the crusty loaves of Central Europe. Traditionally, throughout the world, the harvesting of grain evolved religious festival celebrations, an assurance that basic needs would be fulfilled until the next harvest. There's a deep, centuries-old satisfaction in kneading bread, watching the dough rise to a puffy lightness, taking the beautifully browned breads from the oven, and relishing the satisfying flavor and texture of the first bite.

Breads

American Indian fry bread is a light, puffy round of pastry, excellent with honey

AMERICAN INDIAN FRY BREAD

2 cups flour
4 T instant nonfat dry milk powder
2 t baking powder
2 t salt
1 T shortening
¾ cup warm water
Oil
Honey

Stir together flour, milk powder, baking powder and salt. Cut in shortening until mixture resembles coarse crumbs. Stir in water. Turn onto a floured surface and knead to a smooth ball. Divide dough into eight balls; cover, let set for 10 minutes. On a floured surface, roll each ball into a 6 inch circle. With a finger, make a hole in the center of each circle. Fry, one at a time, in deep hot oil(400°) until golden brown; about 1½ minutes, turning once. Drain on paper toweling. Serve with honey. Makes eight.

French Gougère Bourguignonne, a light delicate bread made with lots of eggs and cheese

CHEESE PUFF RING

¾ cup water
½ t salt
4 T butter
1½ cup sifted all-purpose flour
3 eggs
1 cup cubed Swiss or Gruyère cheese

In a saucepan, combine water, salt and butter; bring to a boil and add flour all at once. Stir constantly over low heat until dough forms a ball and comes away from the sides of the pan. Remove from heat and allow to cool for 5 minutes. Beat in eggs, one at a time, mixing smooth after each is added. Mix in the cheese. Form into a ring on a buttered baking sheet. Bake in a 425° preheated oven until browned, about 25 minutes. Do not open oven during baking or cheese puff ring will fall.

Here is a hearty Middle Eastern bread made with nutritious cracked wheat and wheat flour

CRACKED WHEAT BREAD

1 cup cracked wheat
1 cup water
1 cup milk
2 T sugar
2 T butter
2 t salt
2 cups whole-wheat flour
1 package active dry yeast
2 to 2¼ cups all-purpose flour
Oil
¼ cup sesame seeds

Combine cracked wheat and water in a saucepan; bring to a boil. Remove from heat and stir in milk, sugar, butter and salt; cool to lukewarm temperature. Mix together whole-wheat flour and yeast; add saucepan contents beating until smooth, about 2 minutes at medium speed on a mixer. Add 1 cup all-purpose flour and beat 1 minute; stir in enough remaining flour to make a moderately stiff dough. Turn dough onto a lightly floured surface and knead 10 to 12 minutes. Thorough kneading develops gluten which is essential to good texture and volume. Shape dough into a ball and place in a lightly greased bowl, turning to grease all sides. Cover and let rise in a warm place until doubled, about 1½ hours. Punch down dough and divide into thirds. Shape into balls and let set 10 minutes. Place balls on greased baking sheets and roll into ½ inch thick circles. Brush with oil and sprinkle with sesame seeds. Let rise in a warm place until doubled, about 45 minutes. Bake in a 400° preheated oven for about 15 minutes.

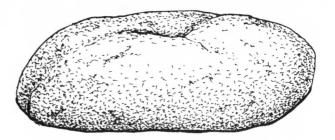

One can hardly pass up crusty French Bread warm out of the oven

CRUSTY FRENCH BREAD

1½ cups warm water
1 package active dry yeast
1 T sugar
2 T salt
4½ cups all-purpose flour
Cornmeal

Pour water into a large bowl; add yeast and stir until dissolved. Stir in sugar and salt. Add flour all at once and stir with a wooden spoon, dough will be stiff and slightly sticky. Cover bowl with a damp towel and let dough rise in a warm place until doubled, about 1 hour. Punch down dough; divide in half. Roll each half on a floured board into a rectangle, 10×14-inches. Roll up, pull to 18 inches and taper ends. Place loaves on a large greased sheet that has been sprinkled with cornmeal. Cut three diagonal slashes on the top of each loaf; cover with a cloth and let rise 1 hour. Brush loaves with water and bake in a 425° preheated oven for 10 minutes. Brush again with water; lower oven to 325° and bake 40 minutes longer. Place on a rack and cool in a draft for a crisp crust.

Arab pocket bread, called Khoubz, is a real treat fresh from the oven

POCKET BREAD

1 package active dry yeast
1¼ cups warm water
½ t salt
3½ cups all-purpose flour
¼ cup toasted sesame seed

In a bowl, blend yeast and water; let stand 5 minutes. Stir in salt and gradually mix in enough flour to form a stiff dough. Turn dough onto a floured board and knead until smooth, about 5 minutes. Add flour as needed to prevent sticking. Cut into 8 equal pieces and cover lightly with a cloth and let rise. On a lightly floured board, shape each piece of dough into a smooth ball; flatten slightly and roll into circles about 4 inches in diameter. Sprinkle each circle with sesame seeds and roll until 5 inches in diameter. Place rounds, seeded side up, about 1 inch apart on greased baking sheets. Cover rounds very lightly with a cloth and let rise in a warm place until puffy looking, about 45 minutes. Bake in a 450° pre-heated oven until lightly browned, about 8 to 10 minutes. Remove bread from oven and wrap individually in foil. Let stand for 10 minutes. When bread is unwrapped tops will have fallen and there will be a shallow pocket of air in their centers. Serve warm with butter. Pocket bread also makes excellent sandwiches; cut in half and stuffed with filling of your choice.

A favorite throughout the Middle East is Lavash, a very-thin, crisp, cracker-type bread

THIN CRACKER BREAD

1 package active dry yeast
1½ cups warm water
1 t salt
2 cups all-purpose flour
2 cups whole-wheat flour
Toasted sesame seeds

Sprinkle or crumble yeast into warm water in a large bowl; stir until dissolved. Add salt. Combine flours and add enough to yeast mixture to make a stiff dough. Turn out onto a floured surface and knead until smooth and elastic, 8 to 10 minutes. Shape into a ball. Place in an oiled bowl and turn to oil top. Cover and let rise until doubled, about 1½ hours. Punch down and let rise again until doubled in bulk, about 30 minutes. Divide dough into 8 equal balls. On a lightly floured board roll out each as thin as possible, forming a circle about 9-inches in diameter. Place one at a time on a baking sheet and prick the entire surface of the dough with a fork; sprinkle with sesame seeds. Bake in a 450° preheated oven until golden brown and crisp, about 5 to 6 minutes, watching closely to prevent burning. Repeat procedure with remaining dough. Cool bread on a rack and store in a covered container in a dry place. Eaten crisp, or sprinkled with water 30 minutes before serving, wrapped in a kitchen towel and set aside to soften. Wrapped around any filling it is uniquely adaptable for sandwiches.

This is a traditional, beautiful, round loaf. Italian Easter bread with an exciting Parmesan fragrance and flavor

PARMESAN BREAD

1 package active dry yeast
⅓ cup warm water
¾ t salt
3½ to 4 cups all-purpose flour
1 cup grated Parmesan cheese
½ t freshly ground black pepper
3 eggs, beaten
2 T olive oil

Sprinkle yeast into warm water; stir until dissolved. Add salt. In a large bowl combine 3 cups flour, grated cheese, black pepper, eggs, olive oil and dissolved yeast; beat until smooth. Stir in enough additional flour to make a stiff dough. Turn onto a lightly floured board; knead until smooth and elastic, about 8 to 10 minutes. Place in an oiled bowl, turning to oil top of dough. Cover; let rise in warm place, about 2½ hours. Punch dough down and let rise again until doubled in bulk, about 1½ hours. Shape into a smooth round ball. Place in an oiled 8-inch round cake pan. Cover with a towel and let rise free from draft, about 1 hour. Brush top of dough with olive oil. Bake in a 350°, preheated oven for 40 to 45 minutes. Remove from baking pan and cool on a wire rack.

Chapaties, a bread eaten in India with highly seasoned curries

WHOLE WHEAT CHAPATIES

2 cups whole-wheat flour
1 t salt
⅔ cup water

Combine flour and salt in a bowl. Gradually stir in water with a fork until a crumbly dough forms. With hands, work dough until it holds together. On a floured board, knead dough with floured hands until it is smooth but still tacky, about 3 minutes. Wrap up dough airtight; let set for 30 minutes. Divide dough into 16 equal pieces; form each into a smooth ball and flatten with hand. On a floured board, roll each ball into a circle about 5 inches in diameter. Just before serving, preheat a dry, heavy frying pan over medium-low heat; place rounds of dough on preheated surface. When bottom is lightly browned, about 2 minutes; press top of bread with a wide spatula, turn and bake until second side is lightly browned, about 2 minutes more. Serve hot.

NOTE:

Chapaties dough may be made ahead and stored in the refrigerator overnight. Circles of dough should be well dusted with flour; stacked, separated by sheets of waxed paper and sealed in a plastic bag.

Black Russian bread is a hearty round loaf made with rye and bran

BLACK RUSSIAN BREAD

4 cups rye flour
3 cups all-purpose flour
1 t sugar
2 t salt
2 cups whole bran cereal
2 T caraway seeds, crushed
2 t instant coffee powder
2 t onion powder
½ t fennel seeds, crushed
2 packages active dry yeast
2½ cups water
¼ cup vinegar
4 T dark molasses
1 ounce unsweetened chocolate, broken into bits
4 T butter
1 t cornstarch
½ cup cold water

Combine rye and all-purpose flour. Thoroughly mix together; 2⅓ cups flour mixture, sugar, salt, bran, caraway seeds, coffee, onion powder, fennel seeds and yeast. In a saucepan, combine water, vinegar, molasses, chocolate and butter; heat slowly until liquids are very warm. Gradually add to dry ingredients and beat for 2 minutes at medium speed on an electric mixer. Add ½ cup flour mixture and beat at high speed for 2 minutes. Stir in enough additional flour mixture to make a soft dough. Turn out onto a lightly floured board; cover and let rise for 15 minutes. Knead dough until smooth and elastic, about 10 to 15 minutes. Dough may be sticky. Place dough in a greased bowl, turning to grease top. Cover and set in a warm place to rise until doubled in bulk, about 1 hour. Punch down and turn onto a lightly floured board.

Divide dough in half and shape each into a ball about 5 inches in diameter. Place each ball in the center of a greased 8-inch round cake pan. Cover and let rise in a warm place until doubled in bulk again, about 1 hour. Bake in a 350° preheated oven for 45 to 50 minutes. Combine cornstarch and water; remove bread from the oven and brush mixture over top of loaves. Return bread to the oven and bake 2 to 3 minutes longer to set the glaze. Remove from pans and cool on a wire rack.

Here is a moist corn bread, with the addition of chopped carrots

CORN-CARROT BREAD

4 T butter
⅓ cup light brown sugar
2 T granulated sugar
2 eggs, separated
2 cups all-purpose flour
1 cup yellow cornmeal
1 T baking powder
1 t salt
½ t baking soda
1 cup buttermilk
¾ cup cooked chopped carrots

Cream butter with both sugars until light and fluffy. Beat in egg yolks. Combine flour, cornmeal, baking powder, salt and baking soda. Add dry ingredients alternately with buttermilk; beginning and ending with dry ingredients. Fold in carrots, then stiffly beaten egg whites. Pour batter into an 8×8×2-inch baking pan that has been greased and dusted with cornmeal. Bake in a 375° preheated oven for 25-30 minutes. Cut into squares and serve hot.

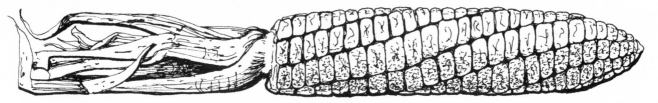

A savory Early Colonial bread; made with cornmeal, rye and whole-wheat flour

Broa is a unique and interesting Portuguese yeast cornbread

EARLY COLONIAL BREAD

½ cup yellow cornmeal
⅓ cup brown sugar
1 T salt
2 cups boiling water
¼ cup oil
2 packages active dry yeast
½ cup lukewarm water
¾ cup whole-wheat flour
½ cup rye flour
4¼ to 4½ cups all-purpose flour

Combine cornmeal, sugar, salt, boiling water and oil; let cool to lukewarm temperature, about 30 minutes. Soften yeast in lukewarm water; stir into cornmeal mixture. Add whole-wheat flour and rye flour; mix thoroughly. Stir in enough all-purpose flour to make a moderately stiff dough. Turn onto a lightly floured surface; knead until smooth and elastic, about 6 to 8 minutes. Place in a greased bowl; turning once to coat all sides. Cover and let rise in a warm place until doubled in bulk, about 1 hour. Punch down, turn out onto a lightly floured surface and divide in half. Cover and let set for 10 minutes. Shape into loaves and place in greased 9×5×3-inch loaf pans. Cover and let rise again until almost doubled in bulk, about 30 minutes. Bake in a 375° oven for 45 minutes. Cap loosely with foil after 25 minutes if the bread is browning rapidly. Remove from pans and cool on a rack.

YEAST CORNBREAD

1½ cups yellow cornmeal, finely pulverized in a blender
1½ t salt
1 cup boiling water
1 T olive oil
1 package active dry yeast
1 t sugar
¼ cup lukewarm water
1¾ cups all-purpose flour

Combine 1 cup of cornmeal, salt and boiling water in a large bowl; stir vigorously until smooth. Stir in olive oil and let mixture cool to lukewarm temperature. In a small bowl, add yeast and sugar to lukewarm water; let stand for a few minutes, then stir to dissolve the yeast completely. Let stand until yeast doubles in bulk, about 10 minutes. Stir into cornmeal mixture. Gradually add remaining cornmeal and 1 cup of the flour, stirring constantly. Form dough into a ball, place in a bowl and drape with a towel. Set aside until dough doubles in bulk, about 30 minutes. Spread remaining flour on a board and knead dough for about 5 minutes. The dough should be firm but not stiff. Pat and shape dough into a round flat loaf and place on an oiled 9-inch pie pan. Drape loaf with a towel and let stand until it doubles in bulk again, about 30 minutes. Bake in a 350° preheated oven until top is golden brown, about 40 minutes. Set on a rack to cool.

Here is a nutritious delicacy made with bran; especially good with a dollop of fresh whipped cream

BRAN GINGERBREAD

5 T butter
5 T sugar
⅓ cup molasses
1 egg
⅔ cup whole bran flour
¼ cup all-purpose flour
1 t baking powder
½ t baking soda
½ t salt
¾ t ginger
½ t cinnamon
⅔ cup boiling water

Beat together butter, sugar, molasses and egg until light and fluffy. Stir in bran and let stand for 5 minutes. Sift together all remaining ingredients, except water; beat into bran mixture. Add water and beat until smooth. Pour into an 8-inch, greased cake pan and bake in a 350° preheated oven for 30 minutes. Serve warm or cool.

A Southern United States recipe for dark and moist bran muffins; made with molasses

MOLASSES BRAN MUFFINS

1 cup whole-wheat flour
¾ cup bran
1 T sugar
⅛ t salt
¾ t soda
1 cup buttermilk
1 egg
¼ cup dark molasses
1 T melted butter

Combine flour, bran, sugar, salt and soda; mix well. Combine buttermilk, egg, molasses and butter. Add all at once to dry ingredients; stirring just enough to moisten flour mixture. Fill greased muffin cups ⅔ full and bake in a 350° preheated oven for 20 to 25 minutes. Makes 12 muffins.

A nutritious, high fiber, quick bread; made with cornmeal, bran and raisins

CORNMEAL BRAN RAISIN BREAD

½ cup butter
6 T sugar
2 eggs
2 cups whole-bran flour
⅔ cup all-purpose flour
1½ t baking powder
½ t salt
6 T yellow cornmeal
¾ cup milk
¾ cup raisins

Beat butter, sugar and eggs until light and fluffy. Stir in bran flour and set mixture aside for 5 minutes. Combine all-purpose flour, baking powder, salt and cornmeal. Gradually add flour mixture and the milk to batter; beating well after each addition. Stir in raisins and spread batter into a greased breadpan. Bake in a 375° preheated oven for 20 minutes. Cool on rack.

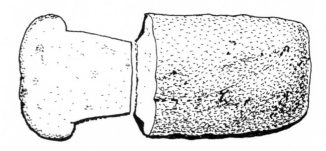

Hawaiian pineapple-nut bread, flavorful with an interesting texture

PINEAPPLE-NUT BREAD

1¾ cup all-purpose flour
2 t baking powder
½ t salt
¼ t soda
3 T butter
¾ cup sugar
3 eggs
1 cup crushed pineapple with juice
¾ cup chopped nuts
Cinnamon

Sift together flour, baking powder, salt and soda. Beat together butter and sugar; add eggs. Stir in half the flour mixture; just until moistened and fairly smooth, do not beat. Add pineapple and juice; stir in remaining flour mixture and fold in nuts. Spoon batter into a greased 9×5×3-inch loaf pan; sprinkle with cinnamon. Bake in a 350° preheated oven until a toothpick comes out clean, about 60 to 70 minutes. Turn out on a rack to cool.

Spoon bread; a favorite in the Southern region of the United States

SOUTHERN SPOON BREAD

2 cups water
1 cup cornmeal
½ t salt
2 T butter
½ cup all-purpose flour
4 eggs, beaten
1 cup milk

In a saucepan, bring water to a boil; gradually stir in cornmeal and salt. Stir one minute, remove from heat; add butter and beat well. Add flour and eggs; continue beating; add milk, beat again. Pour into a very hot buttered 8×8-inch baking dish. Bake in a 450° oven for 25 minutes. Serve hot from baking dish with butter.

Challah, a traditional Jewish Sabbath loaf

CHALLAH

1 package active dry yeast
2 t sugar
⅛ t saffron
1¼ cups lukewarm water
4½ cups sifted all-purpose flour
2 t salt
2 eggs
2 T salad oil
1 egg yolk
4 t poppy seeds

Combine yeast, sugar, saffron, and ¼ cup of the water; let stand for 5 minutes. Sift flour and salt into a bowl. Make a well in the center and drop in eggs, oil, remaining water and yeast mixture; work into the flour. Turn onto a floured surface and knead until smooth and elastic. Place dough in a bowl, brush top with a little oil and let rise for 1 hour. Punch down, cover and let rise again until doubled in bulk. Divide dough into 3 equal parts and with lightly floured hands roll into 18-inch strips. Braid strips and place on a baking pan. Cover with a towel and let rise until doubled in bulk. Brush with egg yolk and sprinkle with poppy seeds. Bake in a 375° preheated oven until browned, about 50 minutes.

Here is a delicious bread made in the United States with sharp Cheddar cheese

CHEDDAR CHEESE BREAD

1 cup lukewarm water
1 package active dry yeast
½ t sugar
3½ cups all-purpose flour
2 t salt
1½ cups grated sharp Cheddar cheese
3 eggs
2 T milk

Combine water, yeast and sugar in a small bowl; let stand until mixture bubbles, about 5 minutes. In a large mixing bowl, combine flour, salt, cheese and 2 eggs. Add yeast mixture and stir until all the liquid has been absorbed. Turn dough onto a lightly floured surface and knead for about 10 minutes. If the dough sticks, add a few spoons of flour and knead until smooth. Place dough in a buttered bowl, cover and let rise until doubled in bulk, about 1 hour. Punch down dough, cover and let rise again, about 40 minutes. Punch dough down again, shape into a loaf and place in a greased 9×5×3-inch bread pan. Beat together remaining egg and milk; brush on loaf. Bake in a 375° preheated oven until bread is golden brown, about 45 minutes. Remove from pan and cool on a rack.

A traditional New England favorite; Boston brown bread made with raisins and molasses

BOSTON BROWN BREAD

1 cup all-purpose flour
1 cup whole-wheat flour
2 T sugar
½ t soda
¾ t salt
⅔ cup raisins
1 egg, beaten
1 cup light molasses
¾ cup buttermilk

Sift together flour, sugar, soda and salt into a bowl; mix in raisins. Combine egg, molasses and buttermilk; blend into flour mixture. Pour into 4 greased soup cans (fill halfway), or a 9×5 inch loaf pan. Bake in a 350° preheated oven until a toothpick inserted in the center comes out clean; 45 minutes for cans, 1 hour for loaf pan.

A nutritious, quick bread, made with rye flour and caraway seeds

CARAWAY RYE BISCUITS

1 cup rye flour
1¼ cups all-purpose flour
1 T baking powder
1½ t caraway seeds
1 t salt
¼ t dry mustard
4 T butter
¾ cup milk

Combine flours, baking powder, caraway seeds, salt and mustard in a bowl. Cut in butter until mixture resembles coarse crumbs. Add milk all at once; mix lightly with a fork until dough forms a ball. Turn dough onto a lightly floured board; roll to ½ inch thick. Cut out biscuits with a 2-inch cutter and place on a greased baking sheet. Bake in a 425° preheated oven until browned, about 12 to 15 minutes. Serve warm. Makes 12 biscuits.

In the Basque Provinces Sheepherder's bread was slowly baked over coal embers; this recipe is baked in a deep Dutch oven

SHEEPHERDER'S BREAD

3½ cups warm water
3 T sugar
3 packages active dry yeast
8 cups all-purpose flour
1 T salt

Stir together, ½ cup water, sugar and yeast in a small bowl; let stand in a warm place until bubbly, about 10 to 15 minutes. In a large bowl, combine yeast mixture and remaining warm water; stir in flour and salt. Knead until smooth, satiny and elastic; about 10 minutes, kneading in enough flour to make a stiff dough. Place dough in a greased bowl turning to grease top. Cover and let rise in a warm place until dough doubles in bulk, about 1 hour. Grease the inside of a 3-inch deep, 10-inch in diameter Dutch oven and its lid. Punch dough down, shape into a round and place in the Dutch oven. Cover with the lid and let dough rise until it just begins to lift up the lid, about 20 to 25 minutes. Bake in a 350° preheated oven for 1 hour and 5 minutes. Check bread several times during baking to make sure lid had not tilted; replace lid squarely on top of bread if it has. Remove lid and bake an additional 10 minutes to allow top of bread to brown. Turn out of Dutch oven immediately to cool.

desserts

Many like to wind up the meal with something sweet. A good dessert can be the happy climax to a meal. The dessert selection depends on how elaborate and filling a meal it is to follow. Nutritionally, if the day's menu has been short on milk, eggs or fruits, the deficiency can be balanced by dessert at dinner. Fruit makes a healthy and popular everyday dessert. Fresh fruits are the simplest and easiest of all desserts to serve, and furnish one of the most wholesome sweets. This is especially true in the summer when fruit is at its best and most plentiful; it need be no more than a perfectly ripe peach or wedge of melon. Europeans traditionally accompany the fruit with assorted cheese. Naturally, the dessert should enhance the meal, supplement a light meal or add a delicate finish to a heavier repast. Occasionally one may want to prepare and serve a special and unusual dessert. Included in this section are dessert favorites from around the world; from the simple chilled rice pudding with almonds and pistachio nuts from India called *Phirni* to a Hawaiian guava chiffon pie with a macadamia nut crust. For most of us dessert is something we are never too full to eat, and a good dessert is a happy ending to an enjoyable meal.

Desserts

A refreshing Spanish dessert is Pastel de Manzana. Apples and mint with a crisp topping

APPLE AND MINT DESSERT

1 T dried mint leaves
1 T cinnamon
4 large tart cooking apples, peeled, quartered and thinly
    sliced
1 cup sugar
1 cup all-purpose flour
½ t baking powder
1 egg
Whipped cream

In a mixing bowl, combine mint and cinnamon. Add apples and toss until slices are well coated. Arrange apple slices in a buttered 8×8×2-inch baking dish. Combine sugar, flour and baking powder. Make a well in the center of flour mix and drop in the egg; mix together with 2 knives until flour has thoroughly absorbed the egg. Scatter mixture over apples; spread and press gently into a smooth layer that cover apples completely. Bake in a 350°, preheated oven for 45 minutes. Serve at room temperature with whipped cream.

A delightful accompaniment to serve with fresh fruit; Persian wine, bread and cheese

CHEESE-WINE PUFFS

4 T butter
4 T whole-wheat flour
1 cup milk, scalded
⅛ t salt
⅛ t black pepper
1 egg yolk, beaten
1 cup diced Monterey Jack cheese
6 slices bread, preferably day-old
White or Rosé wine as needed

Melt butter; add flour and blend well. Stir in milk, salt and pepper. Cook over low heat until mixture is very thick. Remove from heat and stir in egg yolk and cheese. Dip each piece of bread quickly into wine; being careful not to let bread get soggy. Place slices on an oiled baking sheet, spread with cheese mixture; bake in a 400° preheated oven until slightly puffed and browned, about 15 minutes. Cut each piece into 4 strips and serve immediately. Especially good when served with chilled melon.

Palacsinta Földieperrel, a heavenly Hungarian crepe dessert

STRAWBERRY-SOUR CREAM CREPE

Crepe

4 eggs, separated
1 t vanilla
1 cup milk
1 T brandy
1 T melted butter
1 cup all-purpose flour
½ cup chopped walnuts

Mix egg yolks, vanilla, milk, brandy and melted butter with a wire whisk. Add flour and whisk together to make a smooth batter. Beat egg whites until stiff; fold into batter. Heat a lightly greased 7 or 8-inch skillet; pour 3 tablespoons batter into skillet, tilt pan until batter covers bottom. Cook over medium heat until light brown; turn over and brown other side. Cook remaining batter in the same manner. To serve, fill each crepe with a few spoonfuls of strawberry filling and roll up. Spoon some of topping over each crepe and top with chopped walnuts. Makes 12 crepes.

Strawberry Filling

1 quart strawberries
1 T honey
1 T brandy

Combine all ingredients so that strawberries are well covered.

Sour Cream Topping

½ cup sour cream
2 T honey

Mix sour cream and honey together until smooth.

Here is a healthy Spanish candy-like dessert. Figos Recheados, figs stuffed with almonds and chocolate

FIGS STUFFED WITH ALMONDS AND CHOCOLATE

24 whole blanched almonds
12 large dried figs
1 ounce semisweet chocolate, finely grated

Place almonds on a baking sheet and toast in a 350° preheated oven for 10 minutes. Cut stems off figs; with a small spoon make a ½-inch depression in the cut end of each fig. Set 12 almonds aside and pulverize the rest in a blender or nut grinder. Mix pulverized almonds and chocolate; stuff about 1 teaspoon into each fig. Pinch the openings together firmly and arrange figs on an ungreased baking dish; bake for 10 minutes in a 350° oven. Remove and press a toasted almond gently into the opening of each fig. May be served warm or at room temperature.

A smooth, rich gourmet dessert from France

FRENCH SILK CHOCOLATE PIE

½ cup butter
¾ cup sugar
1 ounce square of chocolate, melted and cooled
1 t vanilla
2 eggs
Baked 9-inch pie shell

Cream butter and gradually add sugar. Blend in chocolate and vanilla. Add eggs, one at a time; beating 5 minutes after each addition with an electric mixer on medium speed. Pour into cooled pie shell and chill 1 to 2 hours. May be garnished with whipped cream before serving.

Torta De Garbanzo is an unusual, aromatic Spanish garbanzo bean cake

GARBANZO BEAN CAKE

3 cups cooked and drained garbanzo beans
¾ cup milk
4 eggs, separated
1 cup brown sugar
¼ t ground cloves
¼ t cinnamon
¼ cup rum or brandy

Puree garbanzos with ½ cup milk in a blender; add remaining milk if needed to facilitate blending. Beat egg yolks until thick and lemon colored; add sugar, cloves, cinnamon, rum and garbanzo mixture. Fold in stiffly beaten egg whites. Pour batter into a buttered 13×9-inch baking pan and bake in a 350°, preheated oven until cake is firm in the center, about 40 minutes. Cool and chill overnight. Cut into squares to serve.

For that special occasion, a special dessert; Hawaiian Guava Chiffon Pie with a macadamia nut piecrust

GUAVA CHIFFON AND MACADAMIA NUT PIE

Macadamia Nut Crust

1 cup all-purpose flour
2 T powdered sugar
½ cup butter
½ cup chopped macadamia nuts

Mix together flour and sugar; cut in butter until particles are fine. Stir in nuts. Chill for 30 minutes. Pour into a 9-inch pie pan and press out to form crust. Bake at 425° in the oven until lightly browned, about 8 to 10 minutes. Cool on a rack.

Guava Chiffon Filling

2 envelopes unflavored gelatin
½ cup cold water
4 eggs, separated
1 cup sugar
1 T lemon juice
½ t salt
2 cups guava pulp
Sweetened whipped cream

Combine gelatin and cold water; set aside to soften. Beat egg yolks slightly; add ½ cup sugar, lemon juice, salt and guava pulp. Cook over boiling water until mixture thickens, stirring constantly. Add softened gelatin, stirring until dissolved. Cool until mixture begins to thicken. Gradually beat remaining sugar into stiffly beaten egg whites; fold into thickened mixture. Pour into cooled macadamia nut pie shell; chill until firm. Top with sweetened whipped cream.

Rabarberkräm, a simple delicious Swedish recipe for rhubarb cream

RHUBARB CREAM

4 cups rhubarb, peeled and cut into 1½-inch pieces
2 cups water
4 T sugar
3 T cornstarch
3 T water

In a saucepan, combine rhubarb and water; cook over medium heat until tender. Stir in sugar. Combine cornstarch and water; add to fruit, stirring constantly. Bring mixture to a boil and cook another 3 minutes. Chill before serving. Serve with cream if desired.

An elegant dessert is Viennese Linzer Torte; almond pastry filled with red jam

LINZER TORTE

1½ cups blanched almonds, coarsely chopped
1 cup butter, very cold
1 cup sugar
2 eggs
2 cups all-purpose flour
1½ t cinnamon
⅛ t cloves
2 t cocoa
½ t baking powder
2 to 3 cups raspberry, strawberry or cherry jam

Put almonds and hard butter in a wooden bowl; chop until butter is cut into pieces the size of peas. Add sugar and eggs; mix well. Sift together flour, cinnamon, cloves, cocoa and baking powder; work into butter mixture to make an elastic dough. Remove dough from bowl, wrap in a towel and chill in the refrigerator for at least an hour. Divide dough into 2 parts, one a little larger than the other. Roll out the larger of the 2 portions and fit into a well greased pie pan or spring mold. Fill shell with jam. Roll out remaining dough; cut into strips and arrange a lattice-like top over jam. Bake in a 350° preheated oven for 35 to 40 minutes. Cool and fill lattice openings with more jam.

An excellent Mexican Bread Pudding made with cheese and sliced apples

MEXICAN BREAD PUDDING

2 T butter
3 slices white bread, with crusts, cut into 1 inch squares
1 tart apple, pared and thinly sliced

3 T raisins
1 cup coarsely grated Jack cheese
¼ cup brown sugar, packed
½ cup milk
¼ t cinnamon

Melt butter in a skillet; add bread squares and toss over medium heat until lightly browned. In a 1-quart casserole dish, combine bread squares, apples, raisins and cheese. In a small saucepan, mix sugar, milk and cinnamon over medium heat until sugar dissolves and milk is scalded. Pour over mixture in casserole dish. Bake at 350° in the oven for 30 minutes. Serve hot.

A Lebanese favorite snack made with sesame seeds and walnuts

SESAME NUT SQUARES

2 eggs, separated
⅔ cup honey
3 T nonfat dry milk
¼ cup whole wheat flour
1 cup chopped walnuts
¾ cup sesame seeds
¼ t salt
½ t cinnamon
½ t nutmeg
2 t baking powder

Beat egg yolks until thick and lemon colored. Add honey, dry milk, flour, walnuts, sesame seeds, salt, cinnamon, nutmeg and baking powder. Beat egg whites until stiff but not dry; fold into batter. Spoon into a greased 11×7-inch baking pan. Bake in a 350° oven for 25 to 30 minutes. Cut into squares while warm.

Italian Perie Ripiene, baked pears with walnuts, raisins and wine

STUFFED BAKED PEARS

⅓ cup raisins
¾ cup dry white wine
1½ T sugar
⅓ cup chopped walnuts
4 large pears, cored and cut in half
¾ cup Marsala wine

Soak raisins in white wine for 30 minutes; mix in sugar and walnuts. Arrange pear halves in a baking dish; spoon mixture into the center of each pear. Pour Marsala wine around pears and bake in a 350° preheated oven for 30 minutes, basting occasionally. Serve warm or chilled.

Smaländskostkaka, a Swedish cheese cake made with cottage cheese, cream and almonds

SWEDISH CHEESE CAKE

2 cups cottage cheese
¼ cup all-purpose flour
3 eggs
4 T sugar
2 cups light cream or half and half
½ cup coarsely chopped almonds, lightly toasted

Stir cottage cheese by hand or with a mixer until granular. Add flour, eggs, sugar, cream and almonds. Pour into a greased 10-inch fluted pie pan (or an 8-inch square baking pan); bake in a 350° oven, about 50 to 60 minutes. Cake is done when knife inserted into the center comes out clean. Cool before serving.

Italian wine figs, an elegant yet simple dessert, especially good served with a dollop of sour cream

WHITE WINE FIGS

1 lb. dried figs
1 t grated lemon peel
1 T lemon juice
⅓ cup honey
1 cup dry white wine
Sour cream

In a saucepan, combine figs, lemon peel, lemon juice, honey and wine; bring to a boil. Cover and reduce heat; simmer for 20 to 25 minutes. Serve warm or chilled, topped with sour cream.

Here is a splendid Italian dessert, Ricotta cheese pie

RICOTTA CHEESE PIE

2 cups Ricotta cheese
2 eggs, separated
½ t salt
⅔ cup evaporated milk
¾ cup sugar
3 T cornstarch
3 T lemon juice
9-inch crumb crust

In a bowl, combine cheese, egg yolks, salt and a small amount of the milk; beat until creamy. Add remaining milk, sugar, cornstarch and lemon juice; mix thoroughly. Blend Ricotta mixture into firm, fluffy beaten egg whites. Pour into crumb crust lined pie pan and bake in a 350° preheated oven for 1 hour.

This is a summer dessert from California where both avocados and oranges grow in abundance

ORANGE-AVOCADO MOUSSE

1 large avocado, peeled and cut into chunks
½ cup whipping cream
1 cup orange juice
1 T lemon juice
3 T honey

Combine all ingredients in a blender until very smooth. Pour into a freezer tray or soufflé dish. Freeze until firm, but not hard.

A cool dessert pie for a hot day in Acapulco, Mexico

AVOCADO-LIME PIE

1⅓ cups sweetened condensed milk
1 t grated lime peel
½ cup lime juice
2 egg yolks, lightly beaten
Dash of salt
2 avocados, peeled and forced through a sieve to make
   1 cup
1 baked 8-inch pie crust

Combine condensed milk, lime peel and lime juice in a bowl. Stir in egg yolks and salt. Add avocado, folding in gently until well blended. Turn mixture into pie crust. Chill for several hours.

Cartola is an easy-to-prepare Brazilian dessert made with bananas and Muenster cheese

BANANAS AND CHEESE

4 bananas, peeled
2 T butter
4 slices Muenster cheese
Sugar
Cinnamon

Fry bananas in butter until tender. Wrap each banana in a slice of Muenster cheese and place on an ungreased cookie sheet. Sprinkle with sugar and cinnamon; bake in a 375° preheated oven until cheese is warmed but not melted, approximately 6 minutes. Serve immediately. Traditionally garnished with fresh strawberries when in season.

A classic dessert from the southern United States; apple and molasses pie

SOUTHERN APPLE PANDOWDY

6 apples, pared, cored and cut into small pieces
Cold water
1 cup all-purpose flour
½ t salt
⅓ cup shortening
2 T water
1½ cups molasses
1 t nutmeg
2 t cinnamon
½ t ground cloves

Cover apple pieces with cold water and let stand for 15 minutes. Combine flour and salt; cut in shortening with a pastry blender. Sprinkle with water and mix with a fork until all the flour is moistened; press dough firmly together into a ball with hands. Drain apples and pat dry; turn into a buttered casserole dish. Pour molasses over apples and sprinkle with nutmeg, cinnamon and ground cloves. Roll out pastry to pan size and fit over top of apples. Bake in a 350° preheated oven for about 1 hour. Before serving, break crust into apples.

Phirni, a delicious chilled rice dessert from India; made with almonds and pistachio nuts and flavored with cardamom seeds

RICE PUDDING

½ cup uncooked rice
3 cups milk
2 t cardamom seeds
½ cup slivered almonds
½ cup pistachio halves
½ cup sugar
1 cup evaporated milk

Soak rice in 1 cup milk for at least 2 hours. Place in a blender add cardamom seeds and thoroughly blend. Bring remaining milk to a soft boil and gradually stir in rice mixture. Cook, stirring constantly, until thickened; about 10 minutes. Stir in almonds, pistachios, sugar and evaporated milk, cook 3 minutes longer. Pour into individual serving dishes and sprinkle with more nuts if desired. Cover and chill until serving time.

An Israeli dessert; bananas baked in honey, wine and brown sugar

HONEY-WINE BANANAS

4 bananas, peeled and cut in half
2 T honey
1 t lemon juice
1 cup white wine
⅓ cup brown sugar

Place bananas in a shallow baking pan; drizzle with honey and lemon juice. Pour wine over bananas and sprinkle with brown sugar. Bake in a 400° preheated oven until bananas are tender and glazed, about 15 minutes; basting occasionally.

Here's a simple, delicate, honey custard from Louisiana

HONEY CUSTARD

2 cups milk, scalded
4 T honey
3 eggs, beaten
¼ t salt
⅛ t nutmeg
⅛ t mace

In a bowl, combine milk and honey. Combine eggs and salt and stir into milk and honey. Pour into 4 custard cups; top with nutmeg and mace. Place cups in a pan of hot water and bake in a 375° preheated oven for 40 minutes.

On St. Thomas Island we had a delicious baked dessert; sweet potato pone, delicately flavored with orange

SWEET POTATO PONE

3 cups grated raw sweet potatoes
½ cup soft butter
1 cup brown sugar
¼ t salt
½ cup milk
1 egg, slightly beaten
½ t cinnamon
¼ t nutmeg
2 T grated orange rind
⅓ cup orange juice

Thoroughly blend together all ingredients. Spoon into a shallow baking dish and bake in a 325° preheated oven for 1 hour. May be served warm or cool.

This elegant dessert from Hawaii combines mangoes, papayas, coconut and chopped macadamia nuts

MANGO-PAPAYA AMBROSIA

2 medium, firm ripe mangoes, peeled and cut in bite size
    pieces
2 medium firm ripe papayas, peeled and cut in bite size
    pieces
1½ T lime juice
¼ cup shredded coconut
4 T sour cream
4 T chopped macadamia nuts

Combine mango, papaya, lime juice and coconut. Mix gently and chill for 1 hour. To serve, spoon into dessert dishes and top each with sour cream and nuts.

This is a lovely dessert to serve in the Fall; baked Scandinavian cranberry pudding

CRANBERRY PUFF

2 cups cooked whole-cranberry sauce
⅔ cup sugar
2½ T quick-cooking tapioca
2 eggs, separated
⅛ t salt
¼ t cream of tartar
6 T all-purpose flour

Combine cranberry sauce, ⅓ cup sugar and tapioca in a saucepan; simmer, stirring constantly for 5 minutes. Remove from heat. In a bowl, beat egg whites until foamy; add salt and cream of tartar, beat until stiff. In a second bowl, beat egg yolks until thick and lemon-colored; add remaining

sugar and beat thoroughly. Fold egg yolks into egg whites; fold in flour. Pour cranberry mixture into a 1½-quart casserole dish; cover with batter. Bake in a 325° preheated oven for 40 minutes. Serve warm.

A pie first savored in Canada; pears and orange juice with a crumb topping

PEAR CRUMB PIE

4 pears, peeled, cored and sliced
3 T orange juice concentrate
Pastry for 9-inch one-crust pie
½ cup sugar
⅛ t salt
¾ cup flour
1 t cinnamon
⅓ cup butter

Toss pear slices with orange juice and turn into pastry lined pie pan. Combine sugar, salt, flour and cinnamon. Cut in butter until crumbly. Sprinkle evenly over filling. Bake in a 400° preheated oven for 40 minutes. Serve warm or chilled.

These rich cookies are traditionally served at Mexican weddings

WEDDING COOKIES

1 cup butter
1 t vanilla
2 cups all-purpose flour
1 cup chopped walnuts
Powdered sugar, sifted

Cream butter and vanilla; stir in flour and walnuts. Shape in small balls and place on an ungreased cookie sheet. Bake in a 400° oven for 10 minutes. While still warm roll in powdered sugar. Store overnight before serving. Makes 36 cookies.

Being a Californian, the dessert section would not be complete without this fresh orange cake made with honey and a fresh orange filling

ORANGE-HONEY CAKE WITH ORANGE FILLING

½ cup butter
1 cup honey
2 eggs
¼ cup milk
2 T orange juice
1½ t grated orange peel
2 cups sifted flour
½ t salt
¾ t soda

Cream butter in a large bowl or electric mixer. Continue creaming while adding honey in a fine stream. Add eggs, one at a time, beating well after each addition. Combine milk, orange juice and orange peel. Sift flour, salt and soda together. Add dry ingredients to mixture alternately with liquids; beat after each addition. Pour into 2 buttered 8-inch round cake pans. Bake in a 350° preheated oven 25 to 30 minutes. Cool; fill with orange filling. For a special occasion, frost with whipped cream and sprinkle with toasted slivered almonds.

FRESH ORANGE FILLING

¾ cup honey
2 T cornstarch
¼ t salt
½ cup orange juice
1 T grated orange peel
1 T lemon juice
1 egg yolk beaten
1 T butter

Combine honey, cornstarch and salt in a saucepan. Add orange juice, orange peel and lemon juice.

Cook, stirring constantly, over low heat until mixture is thick and clear. Stir a few spoons of hot mixture into egg yolk and blend into saucepan. Cook. stirring constantly, for 2 minutes longer. Remove from heat and add butter; cool.

A must for apricot lovers are these English honey-apricot pastries

HONEY-APRICOT PASTRIES

Pastry Dough

2 cups all-purpose flour
1 t salt
⅔ cup shortening
5 to 7 T cold water

Sift flour and salt into a mixing bowl; cut in shortening until pieces are the size of small peas. Sprinkle in water, 1 tablespoon at a time until dough begins to stick together. Turn dough onto a lightly floured board; divide in half and shape into 2 balls. Roll out ball to a 12-inch square; cut into 3-inch squares. Place a rounded teaspoonful of apricot filling in the center of each square, spreading slightly. Fold squares diagonally in half, press edges together and prick tops with a fork. Place on an ungreased baking sheet; bake in a 425° oven until tops are lightly browned, about 10 to 15 minutes. Serve warm or cold. Makes 32 pastries.

Apricot Filling

1 cup chopped dried apricots
½ cup chopped raisins
½ cup chopped nuts
¼ cup honey
3 T water

Combine apricots, raisins, nuts, honey and water in a small bowl; mix thoroughly.

Sunflower chews are perfect when just a bit of sweetness is desired; excellent served with fresh fruit

SUNFLOWER CHEWS

¼ cup oil
1 cup brown sugar
1 egg
1 t vanilla
½ cup shelled sunflower seeds
¼ cup shredded coconut
½ cup soy flour
½ cup whole-wheat flour
¼ t salt
1 t baking powder

Thoroughly beat together, oil, brown sugar and egg. Add vanilla, sunflower seeds and coconut; mix well. Sift together soy flour, whole-wheat flour, salt and baking powder; add to mixture, dough will be thick. Spread in a 8×8-inch pan that has been oiled and lightly dusted with flour. Bake in a 350° preheated oven for 20 minutes. Cool on a rack for 5 minutes; turn out and cut into squares. Store in a tight container; with waxed paper between the layers. Makes 25 cookies.

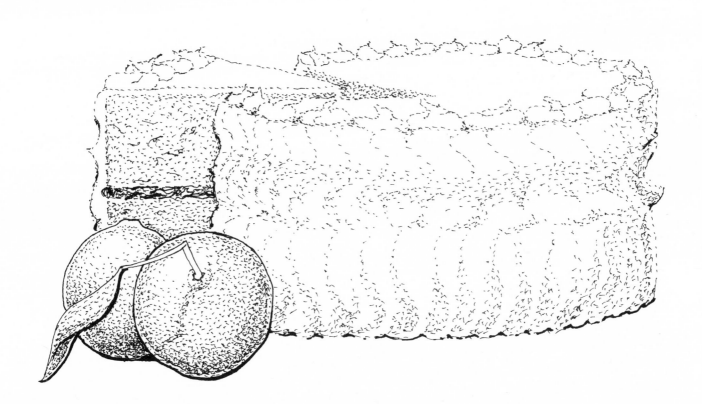

Common Food Equivalents

Food	Amount	Appropriate Measure
Apples	1 pound	3 medium (3 cups sliced)
Berries	1 quart	3½ cups
Beans, dried	1 pound	2 cups (4 to 6 cups cooked)
Cheese		
Cheddar or Monterey Jack	½ pound	2 cups grated
cottage	½ pound	1 cup
cream	3-ounce package	6 Tablespoons
Clams	15-ounce can minced	2 cups shucked
	18 in shells	
Cornmeal	1 pound	3 cups (9 cups cooked)
King Crab legs	½ pound in the shell	1 cup flaked (cooked)
	7½-ounces can	
	6-ounces frozen	
Cream, whipping	½ pint	1 cup (2 cups whipped)
Fish, fillets or steaks	1 pound	2 cups flaked (cooked)
Flour		
all-purpose	1 pound	4 cups
whole-wheat	1 pound	3½ cups
rye	1 pound	4½ cups
Garlic	1 clove	1/8 to ¼ teaspoon garlic powder
Lemon		
juice	1 large lemon	4 tablespoons
peel, lightly grated	1 large lemon	1 to 3 tablespoons
Lobster		
whole	1 pound	1 cup meat (cooked)
	5-ounce can	
tail	½ pound	1 cup meat (cooked)
Milk		
evaporated	14½-ounce can	1⅔ cups
	5⅓-ounce can	⅔ cup
sweetened condensed	14-ounce can	1¼ cups

Food	Amount	Appropriate Measure
Macaroni	4-ounces	1 to 1¼ cups (2¼ cups cooked)
Noodles	4-ounces	1½ to 2 cups (2¼ cups cooked)
Onion	1 medium	1 tablespoon onion powder
Orange		
juice	1 medium	⅓ cup
peel, lightly grated	1 medium	2 tablespoons
Potatoes		
white	1 pound	3 medium (2⅓ cups sliced)
sweet	1 pound	3 medium (3 cups sliced)
Raisins	15-ounce package	3 cups (not packed)
Rice	½ pound	1 cup (3 cups cooked)
Shrimp		
jumbo	1 pound in the shell 15 to 18 shrimp 6-ounce can	⅔ pounds shelled (1⅓ cup cooked)
medium	1 pound in the shell 26 to 30 shrimp	
tiny	1 pound in the shell 60 plus shrimp	
Spaghetti	4-ounces	1¼ cup (2½ cups cooked)
Sugar		
brown	1 pound	2¼ cups (firmly packed)
granulated	1 pound	2 cups
Tomatoes	1 pound	3 medium (3 to 3½ cups chopped)

Index

111

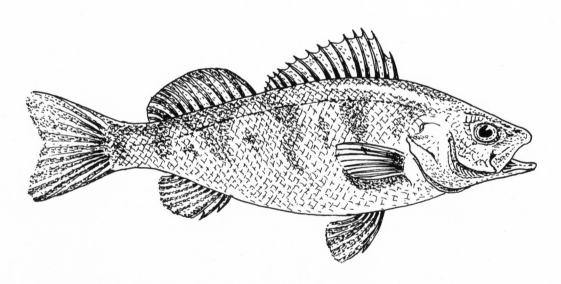